THE COUPLE'S COOKBOOK

Recipes for Newlyweds

Cole & Kiera Stipovich

TEN SPEED PRESS
California | New York

To Chloe, who changed us from a couple to a family. All the midnight oil we burned creating this book can't hold a candle to the light you've brought to our lives. We love you so much.

Contents

Welcome

Hi, and welcome. First of all, congratulations to both of you! Please, come into our office—which also happens to be our home. We work from home, or as we like to put it, we live at work. Our kitchen doubles as a test kitchen, and our living room is also our food photography studio. And when we are not at home writing and photographing cookbooks, we work together as wedding photographers. As such, newlyweds (or almost-weds) are a big part of our daily lives. These people are our clients, yes, but through the process of documenting their weddings, they also often become friends. While it's been more than eight years since our own wedding day, connecting with all types of couples at this unique and exciting stage in their lives means the newlywed chapter still remains a significant part of our lives as well.

After your wedding day, the bliss of your first moments as a married couple remains while your new life together develops its own patina. As life gets busier and more complicated, it's a lovely idea to make simple gestures to remind each other of the lightness of your honeymoon phase. You can think of these moments as "mini dates" that can happen spontaneously on any day and can come in many forms—but it's always about finding a way to connect with each other, make each other laugh, and show each other some affection, even amid hectic schedules or stressful times.

For us, this kind of reconnection most often happens in the kitchen or around the table. Cooking and eating together is one of the most consistent and practical ways we pause our daily schedule in order to have a little "date." It's not always the fancy, elaborate date you might be picturing, but it's the sentiment behind the moment that counts; even a perfectly made peanut butter and jelly sandwich will do.

The ritual of the wedding day points to this secret: All of the couples we work with pause on their wedding day to eat together. Every wedding day goes by like a blur, but we often hear couples say that their wedding meal was a moment of their special day when they remember feeling truly present. If you're reading this cookbook, it's very likely you will want to make cooking or eating together a part of your new married life. We hope the tools and recipes in this book will provide a foundation for the two of you to spend a little quality time with each other over a homemade meal.

And it's not only a way to connect; it's also a way to learn fun new skills together and have a chance to use any of the culinary wedding gifts you may have received. We were thrilled with all the kitchenware we were generously given at our wedding shower—even if we could barely lay out two settings in our tiny apartment, never mind eight! We've learned a lot since then about how to stock and organize our kitchen and how to use the right tools and ingredients to prepare simple, delicious food together and for each other, and we've learned much of it working side by side. We have filled those same plates, which are a daily reminder of our family and friends, with countless meals while creating happy memories in the process. We're sure that no matter your current skill level and regardless of how you set your table, you can gradually and naturally find your own way as a couple in the kitchen.

This book features meals for all parts of the day, with servings for two and sometimes more when the recipe lends itself well to serving a crowd or keeping leftovers. Recipes include prep and cook times and cook's notes to guide you through particulars of special ingredients, plus tips or tools when applicable. This book gives you a neat Rolodex of recipes that you can pull from for various occasions—whether it's an after-work meal on a busy weeknight, a healthy breakfast before running off to work, a decadent breakfast on a slow Sunday morning, a wow-worthy meal when hosting friends, or a dessert to celebrate for any reason.

And a note about the creation of this book. This book was a collaborative effort between both of us through every stage of the process, but the voice you will hear in the recipes is Kiera's. That is, except when you reach the cocktails section. For those recipes we consulted expert Kara Newman, a well-known drinks writer who tells you the ins and outs of putting together your first bar, starting on page 210.

We want to thank you for welcoming this book (and, in a way, us) into whatever place you call home. We hope it resides with you for many happy years.

Tips for the New(lywed) Cook

No two weddings are ever the same because every couple brings their own unique perspective, dynamic, and style to the day. The same rings true as to how you two will live your married (and culinary) life. Cole and I have developed our own way of cooking together, and we wouldn't expect you to follow our approach blindly. The newlywed window is an opportunity to establish your own routine in the kitchen and build a solid foundation to carry you through the years. Discovering your collaborative cooking style is a process that will take time, but here are some fundamental principles to guide you along the way.

If either or both of you are fairly new to cooking, keep an open mind about your skills and abilities. Not many people start off being a fantastic cook, but you can always learn something new, and you may even reveal surprising or hidden talents or passions along the way. Plus, you have the opportunity to learn together or from each other.

"No one is born a great cook, one learns by doing."

—JULIA CHILD

Be Flexible

I believe in discovering each other's strengths and using them to find ways to divide and conquer in the kitchen, but I also would encourage you to swap roles every once in a while. Sometimes life dictates what makes the most sense, but it's most important to keep your minds and communication lines open to discuss what is practical and fair for both of you, especially as situations fluctuate. If you happen to learn that you are not really great at cooking together, consider letting one person do the cooking and the other person can put on some good music and make cocktails. (Also, the designated DJ/bartender might want to offer to be the dishwasher that night. Just saying.)

Start Simple

Start with a simple recipe that speaks to both of you. If you both enjoy it, don't hesitate to work it into a weekly or biweekly dinner rotation. This kind of repetition will also help you learn how to do the dance of cooking together—maneuvering around each other in the kitchen and offering to help the other person. If you can make that time fun and enjoyable for each other, you'll have a stronger foundation to build upon.

Don't Sweat It

If a recipe goes awry, don't get too discouraged. In fact, the biggest flops will one day be funny. I once completely charred some short ribs that I spent a full day planning and preparing. Instead of cooking them in a Dutch oven, I thought I could improvise with the only (flimsy) roasting pan I could find in Cole's apartment. My beautiful adobo-coffee sauce evaporated into black muck, and the ribs that were promised to fall tenderly off the bone had mostly disintegrated off the bone. I was so upset and embarrassed at the time, but Cole ate the whole meal anyway and kept telling me how they were "actually pretty good!" (They weren't.) I learned a little lesson about braising that day and even more about the wonderfully kind person I was dating.

Mise en Place vs. Messy Place

Mise en place is a French culinary term meaning "everything in its place" or "put in place." The idea is that organizing and prepping your ingredients and equipment before you cook will set you up for success, making you more efficient and the experience more enjoyable. If you saw Cole in the kitchen, however, you would see that he seems pretty happy when he is making a big, spontaneous mess. The caveat is that this is when Cole is "riffing" in the kitchen—adding a little bit of this, a little bit of that—which is usually how he cooks. We call this "messy place" cooking, meaning exactly what it sounds like. This carefree

style might speak to you or your partner. If you are married to a "messy place" cook, I advise you to just sit back and let the magic happen. And you should try it sometime, too. Focus on the food and forget the mess.

Following a Recipe

To follow a recipe, especially for the first time, you will probably want to take a more organized *mise en place* approach to set yourself up for success. This is especially true for recipes where everything must come together quickly over the stovetop, such as Udon Stir-Fry with Pork and Baby Bok Choy (page 176) or Cole's Carbonara (page 152). Read through the full recipe two times before you start, walking through the process with a clear mental picture of what your hands are doing and what you smell and see at each step. I like to read the recipe before I shop and again before I cook. Look for tips on ingredients, methods, and other pertinent information in the headnote and cook's notes in each recipe. Take note of the recipe yield (number of servings), as well as the estimated prep time and cook time (inactive and active) so you can plan accordingly. I will also keep a recipe close by while I cook so I can check it to reassure myself I'm on track, particularly when a recipe states a visual cue and a time, which I do a lot in this book. The visual cue is always more important than the time, as ovens and flame power can vary kitchen to kitchen.

PRODUCE

kale   radishes
grapefruit   shallots
oranges   green onion
lemons   asparagus
heirloom tomatoes

MEAT

ground turkey
bacon

DAIRY

greek yogurt
eggs
butter - salted   heavy cream
milk

PANTRY

honey
champagne vinegar
* bread
oats

FREEZER

frozen pineapple
frozen berries

HOME

flowers
dish soap

The Pantry

Before you tackle making dinner, you need to stock your pantry. You will want to purchase some basic staples, but it's important to note that you don't need a picture-perfect, fully stocked pantry to start cooking. Let yourself gradually accumulate ingredients based on what you cook, adding new ones as you add new recipes to your repertoire. I'll give recommendations on what we consider our staples; they're good guidelines but are by no means gospel. But first, these strategies will help you set up and maintain an organized system.

A Thoughtfully Stocked Pantry

A well-stocked pantry should offer variety, but not too much. A concise collection of shelf-stable ingredients will help give you a jumping-off point when planning your next meal, along with seasonal and perishable ingredients that you stock in the refrigerator. Your inventory should emphasize versatile ingredients with the occasional specialty item or seasonal produce. A simple, thoughtfully stocked pantry and refrigerator will make your everyday cooking and shopping easier and more enjoyable and will make storage more manageable.

An Organized Pantry

An organized pantry is a moving target. Store specific dry goods you are continually replenishing in appropriately sized clear storage containers with an airtight seal and a label. Not only is that more visually appealing, but it is also easier to see when you are running low. Use labeled baskets and bins to group similar smaller ingredients when possible, so that everything has a home even as supply levels fluctuate. If you are able to, find a shelf or area where you can store pantry overflow or backup inventory so the cabinets you open on a regular basis are not overcrowded and are easy to scan visually. When you run out of a pantry item, before you add it to your grocery list, you can shop your overflow area first.

Fridge and Freezer Organization

A chaotic, disorganized fridge can quickly become a place where ingredients and perfectly good leftovers go to die. To help keep the fridge under control, store prepped ingredients and leftovers in clear containers with an item label, including the date. Keep masking tape and a marker next to the fridge so you'll be able to make this automatic. Pick a day of the week to take stock of what's there, tossing expired items if necessary. Find a recipe or think of creative ways to use up ingredients on hand, prioritizing perishable ones that are about to deteriorate in freshness. (You get extra points for re-working leftovers!)

The life of so many ingredients can be extended when properly stored in the freezer: meat, sliced bread, nuts, whole blocks of cheese, and very ripe peeled bananas, to name a few. There is a simple method to freezing most foods and preventing freezer burn—just reduce the amount of air that will touch the food. Let warm foods chill completely before freezing. Use freezer-safe storage containers or bags and label, label, label!

Spices

There are so many spices and spice blends available, but it's unrealistic to have them all. This versatile assortment will work with many dishes in this book and help you start (or refine) your spice collection.

Explore the spice section in a gourmet market or a spice shop and indulge in some top-quality spices to see if you appreciate the difference it makes in your cooking. There are also online stores, such as reluctanttrading.com, kalustyans.com, or thespicehouse.com, for convenience.

Refresh your spices every year or so whenever they begin to lose their punch or aroma. Spices will keep best when stored in a cool, dry, dark space—so definitely not near the stove.

Bay leaves: These add an herbal, slightly floral note to soups, stews, or braises. Always remove leaves before serving so that guests don't eat one unexpectedly (or so that your dad doesn't pretend to choke on one, like mine does).

Cardamom: This complex flavor can go in a sweet or savory direction, but I love it best for its use in Scandinavian baking. Combined with butter and sugar in a judicious amount, the piney, floral aroma softens into a warm, sweet, and elusive spice. Think of it as a more sophisticated, sexy cinnamon.

Cayenne: For an instant kick of one-dimensional heat, cayenne is king.

Cinnamon: Ground cinnamon carries an earthy, sweet spice that works well in many baking recipes. For use in savory dishes, try combining it with warm flavors or sweet, starchy vegetables.

Cumin: Ground cumin is a pungent spice with a mildly sweet aroma and earthy flavor. It's essential to many cuisines, including Indian, Latin American, Middle Eastern, and North African, among others.

Nutmeg (whole): Whether used in fall desserts or starchy dinners, freshly grated nutmeg provides a mellow warmth and a hint of sweet spice that rounds out a creamy dish (or cocktail!).

Oregano: Dried oregano has a woodsy, lemony flavor and is most often associated with Italian, Greek, and Spanish cooking styles.

Peppercorns: Freshly ground black peppercorns, like Tellicherry, should be ground right before use—that's how quickly the flavor will diminish. When recipes in this book call for a pinch of freshly ground black pepper, consider it as a couple cranks of the pepper mill.

Red pepper flakes (crushed red pepper): These dried and crushed red chile peppers (including skins, veins, and seeds) can perk up a dish with a medium, sometimes sweet, heat.

Salt: While technically a mineral, not a spice, salt is a powerful seasoning tool that enhances flavor and sweetness and balances bitterness. Keep a coarse kosher salt near the stove for frequent use during cooking as well as a flaky sea salt, fleur de sel, or smoked sea salt for seasoning or finishing dishes. For recipes in this book using kosher salt, I use Morton, which is twice as salty per tablespoon as Diamond Crystal. Salt, either a fine table salt or a fine sea salt, has its own place in certain recipes and shouldn't be equally swapped for kosher salt. Whenever possible, taste and season as you cook and if you're uncertain, err on the side of *less is more*.

Smoked paprika: As the name suggests, this spice will add a warm, mild smoky flavor to your recipes. The sweet smoked version brings the rich smoky flavor without the intense kick of heat.

Fresh Herbs

Fresh herbs are essential to flavorful, fresh-tasting meals. If you have place for even a small herb garden or potted herbs, I highly recommend it. When buying herbs from the market, always look for the freshest-looking bunch.

TENDER HERBS

Basil: This sweet, pungent herb adds flavor to tomato dishes and pesto.

Chives: Chives have a delicate and mild onionlike aroma with a hint of garlic flavor.

Cilantro: While some people insist that cilantro's flavor is soapy, we love its sweet, bright flavor in Mexican dishes or curries.

Dill: These delicate leaves carry a mild, sweet flavor and have a slightly lemony and pungent aroma.

Mint: This sweet, cooling herb will bring a refreshing component to both sweet and savory dishes.

Parsley: Parsley, whether used cooked or raw, will help balance a savory dish with a slightly bitter component and add brightness with a fresh and grassy flavor.

Tarragon: Quintessential in a French béarnaise sauce, this herb is bittersweet—a faint licorice flavor combined with a sweet and delicate finish.

WOODY HERBS

Rosemary: This pungent herb has an assertive piney flavor.

Sage: This bittersweet herb is pungent and earthy.

Thyme: Floral and aromatic, thyme is also woodsy and slightly minty.

To maximize the freshness of cut tender herbs like cilantro, dill, mint, parsley, or tarragon as long as possible, trim the bottom of the stems and remove any less-than-favorable-looking leaves. Wrap gently in dry paper towels and place in a partially closed zippered bag and store in the high humidity drawer of the fridge. For basil, trim the stems and store in a vase at room temperature, loosely covered with a plastic bag, in a bright area but not direct sunlight.

To preserve fresh herbs for later use in cooking, mince the herb and transfer into ice cube trays, then add a small amount of boiling water or olive oil to just cover and freeze. When frozen, transfer the herbal ice cubes to an airtight freezer bag for up to three months.

Dry and Canned Goods

Canned goods are helpful, long-lasting items to keep in your pantry, and many of the dry goods can usually be found in cost-saving bulk bins.

Beans: Canned beans like black beans, cannellini beans, and chickpeas (also known as garbanzo beans) are great for quick meals.

Broth/stock: Homemade broth or stock is the best, but it's good to also keep store-bought on hand in vegetable, chicken, and/or beef varieties. Once you open a box, write the date on it in marker so you know when it's no longer fresh, usually within two weeks.

Canned fish: Tuna and anchovies reside in our pantry based on a, perhaps old-fashioned, notion to keep a shelf-stable source of protein on hand.

Coconut cream: Used to impart rich coconut flavor, this thick and creamy dairy alternative is a great way to enrich smoothies, curries, or soups.

Grains: Arborio or carnaroli rice (risotto), medium-grain white rice, brown rice, farro, thick rolled oats, and quinoa are the grains that I use the most.

Nuts and seeds: Hazelnuts, pecans, shelled pistachios, sliced almonds, pine nuts, and walnuts are always on hand in our house. I like to buy raw whenever possible so that I can control the levels of butter and salt when I roast them myself.

Panko bread crumbs: These Japanese bread crumbs are extra crispy.

Pasta: Long and short varieties—elbows, thick spaghetti, and rotini—are called for in this book.

Polenta/cornmeal/grits: Buy a coarse cornmeal in stone-ground form, and it can be used almost interchangeably for grits and polenta. You'll want a finer ground cornmeal for most baking uses.

Tomatoes: I prefer whole peeled tomatoes.

Tomato paste: I find the tube versions more convenient than the cans.

Condiments, Sauces, and Flavor Enhancers

Oils: You will need a refined neutral-flavored oil for high heat cooking, such as avocado, canola, grapeseed, olive, or safflower oil. A good extra-virgin olive oil, ideal for salads or finishing dishes, should be creamy, with a pleasant, pungent aroma that finishes with a distinctive peppery bite. Store cooking oils in a cool, dark place.

Vinegars: We have a fairly large collection of vinegar varieties in our pantry—red wine, sherry, champagne, white wine, apple cider (unfiltered), rice (unseasoned), balsamic, and malt. (This many vinegars isn't necessary—it's more of a personal problem.) The acidic bite of vinegar is essential for balancing flavors in sauces and dressings.

Capers: Use capers or just a dash of the caper juice to add a bright, salty acidity to anything that could benefit from a hint or burst of pickle brine.

Chili paste: Keep a chili paste as a flavoring agent for sauces, dips, or spreads to add spice to your cooking. Gochujang, harissa, sambal oelek, or sriracha all have subtle differences that you may enjoy exploring.

Gochujang is a spicy, sweet fermented Korean chili paste with umami packed heat.

Harissa is a Tunisian red chili pepper paste made with warm, earthy spices like cumin, coriander, and caraway seeds. You can mix it with aioli or olive oil to pair with anything from roasted vegetables to an egg sandwich.

Sambal oelek is a Southeast Asian chili paste with a slightly chunky texture and simple, clean delivery of heat without any other overpowering flavors.

Sriracha is a chili paste with a smooth texture, strong garlic and vinegar flavor, and hint of sweetness.

Fish sauce: Fish sauce is a pungent, funky ingredient that once incorporated into a dish adds a salty, caramel-like, umami flavor.

Honey: When possible, seek out local, organic honey from farmers who practice sustainable beekeeping.

Hot sauce: We encourage you to find your favorites among the endless hot sauce varieties. I like a cayenne-based hot sauce for simple, clean heat when a brand is not specified in our recipes.

Ketchup: This sweet and acidic tomato condiment is a must-have. Sometimes the smooth reliable bottle of Heinz 57 does the trick, but don't be afraid to try newer, more natural options. Brands like Sir Kensington's feature a little more texture and a less processed flavor.

Maple syrup: Look for 100 percent pure maple syrup and choose from Grade A color gradients that range from light amber to dark amber, which will correspond to the maple flavor intensity.

Mayonnaise: This creamy, emulsion of egg and oil cut with acidity from vinegar or lemon juice should taste fresh and balanced. While there isn't anything quite like homemade aioli (page 24), sometimes store-bought is more convenient.

Miso paste: Japanese in origin, this is a fermented mixture of soybeans mixed with a grain and koji (a safe type of mold that grows on rice), packs an umami punch that you will want in your arsenal. It's salty, complex, and funky (in a good way) and should be added gradually, as it can be powerful.

Molasses: Molasses is a thick, sticky syrup with sweet, umami flavor used in baking and savory recipes alike. A light molasses will work best for most baking recipes, but you can also use dark (robust or full flavor) molasses to bake a rich gingerbread cookie. Sulfured or blackstrap versions will be too bitter for baking. In savory dishes, molasses can be used in barbecue sauces or stir-fry marinades.

Mustard: Dijon should have a bold tangy flavor with a pleasant but wrinkle-your-nose heat and a smooth texture that works well in vinaigrettes. Alternatively, a country-style or whole grain mustard has a similar flavor to Dijon, but the seeds add texture and a nice bite that we like in sandwiches.

Soy sauce: One of the easiest ways to add a savory umami and saltiness to sauces and marinades is with soy sauce. Not just for Asian cuisine, soy sauce is a useful ingredient in meat loafs, stews, and barbecue recipes.

Worcestershire sauce: This savory meat enhancer adds a dose of vinegary, salty fermented flavor, which comes from anchovies, but is tempered with an earthy sweetness.

Baking Ingredients

Throughout this book you will see baking ingredients listed in imperial measurements (cups, tablespoons). In some places you will also see metric measurements in grams; these are for recipes that require more precision, so if you have a kitchen scale this is an indicator that you should use it!

Active dry yeast: Mostly used for leavening bread doughs, this ingredient is easy to keep in stock for when the need arises (or "knead a-rises"). Store in the refrigerator and always check the expiration date before using.

All-purpose flour: As the name suggests, this is the best option for varied uses. Other types of flour are called for in this book, but it's wise to always have "AP" flour on hand. Store in a cool, dry location, preferably in an airtight container.

Baking powder: Baking powder is a chemical leavening agent that makes baked goods rise. While it is similar to baking soda, the two are definitely not interchangeable. Store in a cool, dry place and mind the expiration dates.

Baking soda: Like baking powder, baking soda is a chemical leavening agent that makes baked goods rise, but is about three times as potent and is activated by wet acidic ingredients. Be mindful of the expiration date because age can make it less effective. Although it's regularly stored in refrigerators as an odor-absorbing tool, it should be stored in a cool, dry place when used for baking.

Chocolate: In baking, I prefer to chop from a good-quality chocolate bar (with at least 60 percent cacao) instead of chocolate chips, which generally have added preservatives that affect the way they melt.

Espresso powder: Also called instant espresso, this is a "secret ingredient" in so many of my baking recipes—especially ones containing chocolate. A small amount of it will enhance the complex chocolate flavors without imparting a strong coffee flavor. When you *do* want to add coffee flavor, but don't want to alter the liquid composition of a batter, sauce, or rub in the form of brewed coffee, use more than a teaspoon of espresso powder.

Vanilla bean paste: Pure vanilla bean paste or, even better, Madagascar bourbon vanilla bean paste is another one of my go-to baking ingredients. I rarely need to buy vanilla pods and scrape out the beans when this magic in a jar exists. Its rich vanilla flavor with specks of vanilla seeds is particularly fantastic in frostings and ice cream. Just substitute a portion or the full amount of vanilla extract.

Essential Kitchen Equipment

Many of you reading this might be either in the midst of registering for wedding gifts or admiring the towering stack of presents you now have to find space for in your home. I still have vivid memories of Cole beep-beep-beeping his way through department stores with that registry price gun; he definitely had a more-the-merrier approach, whereas I tried to stress the importance of asking only for things we really needed. We remained in those two camps throughout our engagement, but once it came time to fit all those generous gifts into our tiny apartment, Cole saw the light.

For many of us, cooking feels complex enough, so unless you are really excited about a particular technique or tool, let your equipment remain simple. You can accomplish a lot with the basics, and it makes sense to let how and what you cook dictate the kitchen equipment that is most essential. You can gradually add more nice-to-have items once you figure out where your specialty cooking interests lie. From a long-term budget standpoint, it's best to focus on well-made, high-performing tools that will last you long throughout your culinary journey ahead. These are the pieces of kitchen equipment that I believe are the most versatile, helpful items you will learn to trust and enjoy in the kitchen.

An asterisk (*) indicates the most essential items, meaning we use them the most and we would prioritize them in both terms of budgeting funds and space. Others are nice to have but might not be necessary for you, based on how you cook and how you want to budget said funds and space.

Utensils

All these utensils could live in one or two jars or utensil holders next to the stovetop. There may not be room for them all in one jar specifically, but these are the smaller tools that are high-use items to be kept within reach.

Potato masher: In addition to mashing potatoes, you can use this tool to manually break down any large semisoft foods, such as whole peeled tomatoes or avocados, into a rough, chunky mixture or rough paste. (A potato ricer also does this job, arguably better, but it is a much bulkier item to store and use.)

*Spatulas: Having both a small and a medium-large spatula will come in handy. An all-silicone spatula (one material with no seam) is heat-resistant, nonstick friendly, and easy to clean. I prefer ones with a straight side for better bowl-and-corner scraping.

*Spoons: There are many types of spoons for all kinds of niche uses. A single multipurpose cooking spoon (often called a serving or basting spoon) will get you through the day, but it's nice to also have a slotted spoon, a wooden spoon, and a nonstick spoon (silicone-coated), as well as a deep ladle available.

*Tongs: A pair of silicone-tipped tongs are great for nonstick cookware and most everything else. For outdoor grilling, make sure you have a second pair of long all-metal tongs.

*Turners: One large metal turner, one medium (but thin) silicone-coated turner, and one slotted turner (fish spatula) will cover all your "flipping" needs for various food items and cooking surfaces.

*Whisks: You will need wire whisks (all-purpose, such as balloon or French) in 10- and 15-inch versions for mixing smaller and larger quantities of eggs, custards, sauces, and so on.

COLANDERS AND STRAINERS

*Salad spinner: Technically this one only comes out for salad nights, but it's a rough assignment to dry your washed lettuce without it. As a space-saving bonus, it can serve double duty as a multiuse bowl and a colander.

*Sieve/strainer: I use a fine-mesh metal strainer often. You'll want one mini conical one (3 inches) and one large one (7 to 9 inches). Be a minimalist and also use the large one for sifting.

MIXING AND MEASURING EQUIPMENT/ PREP TOOLS

*Dry measuring cups (scoops): A sturdy set of four stainless steel measuring cups that stack is easy to use and store.

*Liquid measuring cups: Pyrex measuring cups are heatproof and the proper way to measure for liquid ingredients. For measuring accuracy, set the cup on a level surface and get down to eye level to view the markings on the side of the cup (really!). Silicone measuring cups that can withstand very high temperatures are also useful, and their flexible sides make them great tools for pouring.

*Measuring spoons: A set of four or five stainless steel measuring spoons with easy-to-identify markings (preferably etched so they won't fade) is essential. My personal favorite is a magnetic set that comes apart and stacks away conveniently.

*Mixing bowls (stainless steel): A set of three nesting stainless steel bowls will get lots of use. Stainless steel is lightweight can be tossed around with abandon, and is heatproof so it is great for setting on top of hot water for a makeshift double boiler.

Mixing bowls (glass): As you prep your food, chopping and measuring and separating ingredients, a set of 5 to 10 glass nesting bowls will help you get organized. Look for glass bowls that are heat and shatter resistant, such as borosilicate or tempered glass.

*Food storage containers: I prefer glass but I also keep a very basic set of clear plastic deli containers in varying sizes (8 ounces, 16 ounces, 32 ounces) that all use the same size lid. Stick to coordinating sets that will stack and store away nicely.

TOOLS FOR CUTTING

Quality, sharp knives are essential to a proper and enjoyable cooking experience. You can find your way through this book and most situations with just a couple knives—the chef's knife, a paring knife, and a serrated bread knife.

Chef's knife (8 or 9 inches): A chef's knife is very personal. You can find many options in many price ranges, but be sure to pick a good-quality knife. Most important, you shouldn't choose a knife without holding it to feel its overall heft, the distribution of weight in your hand, and how comfortable and appropriate the size is for you. Take care of your knife by having it sharpened regularly. Wash and dry it after each use—don't leave it in the sink. And please, don't cut directly onto a glass, marble, or metal surface.

Paring knife: A small utility knife is needed for chopping smaller ingredients or for more control with its sharp tip.

Serrated bread knife: A long serrated knife will be able to saw gently and cleanly through crusty rustic loaf with tender crumb interiors, pastries, and a carefully composed sandwich. You may also want a smaller serrated knife for slicing tomatoes.

Cutting boards: One small and one large cutting board or chopping block will serve you well. We use a large, hefty wooden board made of maple that we often leave out on the counter and a few smaller wooden ones that we stow away. Wood does require a little maintenance (food-grade mineral oil), but a soft wood is easier on your knives and will last many, many years if you take good care of it.

Kitchen shears: Consider shears the Swiss army knife of the kitchen. Find a well-made, quality pair that is strong enough to cut up poultry and that separates for easier cleaning.

SLICERS, GRATERS, AND PEELERS

Grater: An extra coarse grater in a paddle style for shredding cheeses will store nicely and is easier to clean than a box grater.

Mandoline: You can get by without one, but there is no real substitute for the speed, quality, and consistency you can achieve with a mandoline. I also recommend using a hand guard when possible and/or getting a protective glove if you are as accident-prone as I am.

Peeler: A y-peeler or a straight peeler for prepping fruits and vegetables will be necessary for many recipes. Many professionals use the Kuhn Rikon original Swiss peeler for its sharp carbon-steel blade, ease of use, and affordability.

Zester: A zester (or rasp grater) is a versatile, compact tool intended for zesting citrus, but its uses don't stop there. We regularly use ours to finely grate hard cheeses, to grind whole spices (nutmeg, cinnamon), or to incorporate the flavors of ginger, garlic, or shallots as a minced paste. It's even come to the rescue to scrape off burnt sections of toast or cookies.

Seasoning and Oil Dispensers

Like your cooking utensils, you'll want to have these on the countertop by the stove for easy access.

Oil container: A glass or ceramic container with a pour spout is nice to have to keep your favorite cooking oil(s) easily accessible.

Pepper mill: A pepper mill should be durable and easy to fill and include an adjustable grinding mechanism. An attractive design doesn't hurt either, as it may end up on your serving table.

Salt cellar: A small ceramic or wooden container with a lid near the stove is convenient for grabbing a pinch of salt. I keep one for cooking salt and one for finishing salt.

Bakeware

Baking dishes: Square and rectangular baking dishes are very versatile for casseroles. Take precaution with glass and some ceramic dishes as they have the potential to shatter or crack when used in very high heat, such as under the broiler. There are beautiful enameled stoneware options that are oven-, broiler-, microwave-, freezer-, and dishwasher-safe—perhaps the best of all worlds.

Baking sheet pans: Also referred to as half-sheet pans, a good commercial-quality rimmed aluminum pan will be your best friend for roasting vegetables, baking cookies or scones, or even using as a tray for gathering ingredients during meal prep. They stack and nest so they take up minimal storage space. Half-sheet pans are the standard size for home use, but when cooking for two, it's nice to also have quarter-sheet pans.

Cake pan/baking pans: Two 6- or 8-inch round cake pans will serve you well over the years for most celebration cakes. If you are an avid baker, you will likely also want square and rectangular aluminum baking pans for brownies and beyond.

Loaf pan: An aluminum loaf pan is usually used for breads and meat loaf. A loaf pan is also the perfect size for making a small batch casserole.

Pie pan/dish: You can opt to use a pie or tart pan (metal) or pie dish (glass or ceramic). A serious pie maker will prefer metal for achieving a neatly shaped dough and a nice evenly browned crust. Dough tends to slip around in glass, and glass also has potential to shatter when going from being chilled to the oven. Ceramic makes for a beautiful presentation but is the slowest to bake.

*Wire rack: Choose a sturdy, stainless steel wire rack with a small grid to cool delicate baked goods. An oven-safe rack can be set over (or ideally inside) a rimmed baking sheet can be used as a makeshift roasting rack or crisper tray. This setup is also ideal to let excess oil drain off of foods.

Pots and Pans

*Cast-iron skillet: A 9- or 10-inch cast-iron skillet will be a kitchen workhorse. It needs a little extra preheating time, and you should use extra precaution when grabbing the handle as it can get very hot. Most important, dry it thoroughly (until "bone dry," as my dad once taught me) and promptly after washing by hand. To wash, use a soft cloth or nonabrasive brush and only a mild soap when necessary. "Season" your skillet regularly with a small amount of a neutral cooking oil while still warm, and it will be virtually nonstick and last a lifetime.

Cast-iron grill/griddle pan: Buy a grill and griddle pan separately if you don't need both or would prefer either pan to have a long handle, but a large reversible option is nice for its size and dual functionality.

*Dutch oven or French oven (6 to 8 quarts): A deep, enamel-coated pot with a lid, like Le Creuset or Staub, is great for even browning and essential for meals like stews and braises and any dish that benefits from a long, slow simmer or goes from stovetop to oven.

*Nonstick frying pans/skillets (8, 10, or 12 inches): It's nice to have one smaller and one larger nonstick frying pan for a variety of jobs. Realistically though, a 10-inch nonstick frying pan is our one-size-fits-mostly-all pan. A nonstick surface is ideal for eggs and browning delicate foods, and it keeps cleanup elbow-grease-free. Use soft, nonabrasive tools while cooking with or cleaning these pans.

*Stainless steel skillet/frying pan: A 10-inch stainless steel skillet with slanted sides is ideal for browning and searing and is ultra-durable. A stainless steel lined cooking surface blended with a copper base is the best of both worlds for optimal heat conduction and user friendliness. Clean the tougher messes with a thorough soaking in warm, soapy water, then use Bar Keepers Friend (or a similar cleaner) and scrub with a nonabrasive sponge.

Stainless steel sauté pan with lid: A sauté pan is similar to a skillet, but with straight sides and slightly deeper. An 11- or 12-inch sauté pan with a 3- to 4-quart capacity would be a nice-to-have pan, but we find we can achieve the same goals in other pots and pans.

*Stainless steel saucepan with lid: A 1- to 2-quart saucepan is essential for basic cooking. A 4-quart saucepan is nice to have for larger quantities, too.

*Stockpot with lid (7 to 12 quarts): You will need a stainless steel stockpot for cooking pasta. A 7- or 8-quart stockpot is needed to cook 2 pounds of pasta, which you will likely want to do on occasion. A 12-quart (or up to 16-quart) stockpot may become necessary if you are feeding a big crowd, but see if you can get by without it if space is limited.

Wok (14 inches): A wok is used for a variety of cooking techniques, but mostly you'll be bringing it out for stir-frying. Traditionally it is made of carbon steel because it's an inexpensive material that heats very quickly and is surprisingly lightweight.

Small Appliances

*Electric teakettle or standard teakettle: I like the simple romance of a whistling teakettle over a fire, but we registered for an electric teakettle at someone's recommendation and we haven't looked back since.

Food processor: The food processor is another item you could live without, but nothing replaces what a good processor can do. I started with mini 4-cup-capacity food processor for chopping and blending small quantities and eventually added a 14-cup capacity for (much) bigger jobs and more specialized slicing and dicing options.

High-powered blender: I didn't say Vitamix, but I meant it. This is a high-ticket item, but people who have one (ourselves included) use it often and swear by it's power and durability. I am putting it on here because many of our newlywed clients said this is one of their favorite registry gifts.

Immersion blender: In lieu of a Vitamix, I would recommend a good-quality immersion blender over a standard blender for storage reasons and for easier cleanup. Our All-Clad one has served us very well.

Stand mixer: A stand mixer will be indispensable if you are an avid, frequent baker. I have gotten so many miles out of my Kitchen Aid Pro Series (yes, it's "mine" not "ours"). If you are going to be a longtime user of your mixer, a model with the bowl-lift has a more powerful motor and greater capacity, and will be worth the investment.

Toaster: If you love bread and bagels, find a two-compartment toaster that will toast evenly and has wide openings for big, doughy bagels.

Waffle maker: You can live without waffles, I think. I consider waffles one of those foods that truly brings joy and turns breakfast into a special occasion. I recommend a waffle maker that flips.

Baking and Pastry Tools

Bench/dough scraper: Use this tool to cut and lift dough and clean work surfaces.

Biscuit cutter: Don't use an upside-down glass or a mason jar as a kitchen hack in lieu of biscuit cutters.

You'll use them at some point, if not for biscuits, then for cookies, Play-Doh, egg-in-a-hole toast, or even a fried egg.

*Digital instant-read thermometer: A digital instant-read thermometer is useful for meat as well as for bread making or to discreetly check the internal temperature of a deep casserole dish.

Digital kitchen scale: If you are serious about baking, especially for the bread recipes in this book, I strongly encourage you to get one for weighing ingredients.

Ice cream scoop: I like both the classic Zeroll version as well as the kind with a spring-loaded release. These scoops are also great for uniformly transferring batter into muffin pans or for shaping cookie dough or even meatballs.

Offset spatula: A medium-size offset spatula will be useful for frosting cakes or smoothing out a batter.

Rolling pin: If pie, pastry, or cookie making are in your future, you'll want a wooden rolling pin. I like a straight cylinder with no handles, but a tapered rolling pin for even thickness (cookies) is sleek and easier to control and maneuver, especially around edges (pie and pastries).

Specialty Tools and Gadgets

You may wish to add these items only as the need arises, especially if short on storage.

Baking stone

Can opener

Cheesecloth

Cheese plane/slicer

Citrus reamer/juicer

Corer

Culinary torch

Digital kitchen timer

Egg ring

Funnel

Meat tenderizer/mallet

Mortar & pestle

Oven thermometer

Pastry brush

Pizza peel

Waiter's corkscrew wine/bottle opener

Breakfast & Brunch

Grilled Green Tomatoes and Burrata Toast

Green tomatoes are actually just unripe tomatoes, so they have a notable firmness to them. This makes them great for frying, cooking—or even grilling, which lends a lovely sweetness to their distinctive tartness. It's possible you won't be able to find them in the grocery store or farmers' market, but it's worth checking or asking around. You will have the best luck harvesting them fresh from the garden. If you don't have a garden, try befriending someone who does have one! If you can't find green tomatoes, try a green type of heirloom tomato and skip the grill pan process.

2 slices rustic country bread, cut 1 inch thick

1 large garlic clove, halved

1 tablespoon extra-virgin olive oil, plus more for drizzling

¼ teaspoon kosher salt

Pinch of freshly ground black pepper, plus more as needed

1 to 2 green tomatoes (firm, unripe tomato), stem removed and cut into ¼-inch-thick slices

4 ounces burrata, at room temperature

4 leaves basil, thinly sliced (for garnish)

Flaky sea salt (optional)

Preheat the oven to 350°F.

Place the bread slices on a baking sheet and toast in the oven until warm and starting to crisp up slightly, 3 to 5 minutes. Remove from the oven and gently rub the garlic over the warm bread; discard the clove. Drizzle the bread slices with 1 tablespoon of the olive oil and season with salt and pepper. Set aside.

Meanwhile, in a grill pan over medium heat, cook the tomatoes for 2 to 3 minutes per side, until lightly charred but still firm.

Spread half of the burrata over each slice of seasoned toast, then top with the grilled tomatoes. Garnish with the basil, then drizzle with additional olive oil. Season with flaky sea salt, if using, and additional pepper to taste.

Huevos Rancheros

Every couple has particular recipes that somehow end up within the purview of one or the other. In our household, Cole (the Californian) is more at home with Mexican-style dishes. Between Cole's parents, Cole's dad has taken ownership of this fresh and hearty breakfast. (Although, truth be told, Cole's mom taught his dad how to make it in the first place.) While this is not either of Cole's parents' exact recipe, it is built from delicious memories. It's our hope that it will fall under new ownership in your household and that you'll create breakfasts that linger in memories for years to come.

¾ cup canned black beans

1 tablespoon canola or neutral oil

4 small corn tortillas

1 cup shredded Monterey Jack cheese

1 tablespoon salted butter

4 eggs

¼ teaspoon kosher salt

¼ teaspoon freshly ground black pepper

½ cup Pico de Gallo (page 157) or store-bought

Hot sauce (optional)

½ ripe avocado, cubed

3 tablespoons coarsely chopped cilantro

3 tablespoons thinly sliced green onions

Cook's Note: It's a bit of a dance to cook the eggs and heat the tortillas at the same time, so make sure to have your ingredients at the ready.

In a saucepan over medium-low heat, add the black beans and heat until warm. Set aside.

In a large nonstick skillet over medium-high heat, add the oil. Once the oil is hot, add the tortillas and cook for 1 minute, or until warm. Flip the tortillas and cook for an additional 30 seconds. Transfer the tortillas to a baking sheet, overlapping two tortillas slightly to create a pair of tortillas in the shape of the number 8. Evenly distribute ¾ cup of the cheese onto the two pairs of overlapped tortillas. Set aside.

Arrange an oven rack 4 inches from the broiler and preheat the broiler.

In a nonstick skillet over medium heat, add ½ tablespoon of the butter and cook until sizzling. Crack 2 of the eggs and gently add them side by side to the skillet. Season with a pinch of the salt and pepper. Turn down the heat to medium-low, and cook, covered, for 1 to 2 minutes, until the yolks are opaque but not cooked through.

While the eggs are cooking, use a slotted spoon to evenly distribute the black beans and pico de gallo onto the tortilla pairs, and add the hot sauce to taste, if using. Remove the pan from the heat. Gently slide the eggs out of the pan and onto one of the tortilla pairs. Repeat the process for cooking the remaining 2 eggs and place them on the other tortilla pair. Evenly distribute the remaining ¼ cup of cheese over the eggs.

Place the baking sheet with the assembled tortillas in the oven and broil for 30 seconds to 1 minute, until the cheese on top has melted. Using a spatula, carefully transfer each set of tortillas to a plate. Distribute the avocado, cilantro, and green onions evenly over the top.

Savory Dutch Baby with Leeks, Pancetta, and Goat Cheese

If you have never had a Dutch baby, you are in for a real treat. Imagine it as a pancake and a popover, but on steroids. This savory version is welcome at the table almost any time of day, and you can play with substituting your favorite cheese, meat, or vegetables. It is light but satisfying, not to mention really impressive as you take it all puffy and golden out of the oven. Baking and serving right in the skillet makes it perfect for casual meals.

3 leeks

4 ounces pancetta, thickly sliced

3 eggs

¾ cup milk

¼ teaspoon freshly ground black pepper

¾ cup all-purpose flour

2 tablespoons salted butter

3 ounces goat cheese, crumbled

2 ounces Parmesan cheese, grated

2 tablespoons chopped flat-leaf parsley

Preheat the oven to 400°F.

Trim the roots and dark green tops from the leeks and discard. Cut the stalks crosswise into about ¼-inch rounds, and separate the layers of each round into rings. Place the leek rings in a colander and rinse thoroughly, making sure any soil or sand has been removed. Pat dry with a paper towel and set aside.

In a 9-inch cast-iron or oven-safe skillet over medium heat, add the pancetta slices in a single layer and cook until crisp, about 5 minutes on each side. Transfer the pancetta to a plate lined with paper towels, reserving the pancetta drippings in the skillet.

Add the leek rings to the skillet and sauté over medium heat until softened and golden, 5 to 7 minutes. Transfer the leeks to a plate and set aside.

In a blender or stand mixer fitted with the whisk attachment, add the eggs, milk, and pepper and mix until well combined. Gradually add the flour, ¼ cup at a time, and blend or mix until just incorporated.

Wipe the skillet that contained the leeks clean, then add the butter. Place the skillet in the oven until the butter has melted, 3 to 5 minutes, watching carefully so as not to burn the butter. Carefully remove the hot skillet from the oven, swirl the butter to coat the skillet, and add the egg mixture to the skillet. Working quickly, evenly distribute the pancetta, leeks, cheeses, and parsley on top of the egg mixture.

Place the skillet back into the oven and cook until puffed and golden on the edges, about 20 minutes.

The Dutch baby will deflate when removed from oven. Cut into wedges and serve immediately.

MAKES 2 SERVINGS

Prep Time: 15 minutes
Cook Time: 35 minutes

Spicy Sweet Potato and Ham Hash with Spanish-Style Aioli

A hearty cowboy breakfast skillet with layers and variety. For a vegetarian version, you could substitute the ham with lightly sautéed spinach. The Spanish-style aioli recipe will make almost twice as much as you'll need, but it can be a versatile condiment to spread on a breakfast sandwich or a dip for steamed asparagus or seared salmon.

Aioli

3 or 4 garlic cloves, minced

Pinch of kosher salt

1 egg yolk

1 tablespoon water

2 teaspoons lemon juice

Pinch of freshly ground black pepper

½ cup neutral oil (such as canola, safflower, avocado, or extra light olive oil)

½ cup extra-virgin olive oil

Hash

2 teaspoons salted butter

4 to 6 ounces smoked ham, from a mini ham or half ham, cut into ¾-inch cubes

2 tablespoons canola oil

2 small sweet potatoes, peeled and cut into ½- to ¾-inch chunks

1 small yellow onion, coarsely chopped

To make the aioli: Add the garlic to a mortar and sprinkle with salt. Using a pestle, smash the garlic into a fairly smooth paste. Transfer the garlic paste to the bowl of a food processor. Add the egg yolk, water, lemon juice, and pepper. With the food processor running, slowly drizzle in the neutral oil, scraping down the sides as necessary, and blend until all of the oil is emulsified. Transfer the garlic and egg mixture to a bowl. Whisking constantly, slowly drizzle in the extra-virgin olive oil. (If making ahead, store in an airtight container in the refrigerator for up to 1 week.)

To make the hash: In a large cast-iron skillet over medium heat, melt the butter and cook the ham until lightly browned. Remove the ham from the skillet and set aside.

Add the oil to the skillet. When the oil is hot, add the potatoes and cook, stirring occasionally, until they begin to brown, about 7 minutes. Add the onion, stirring to combine, and cook, flipping occasionally, until the potatoes are tender and golden brown on all sides, about 20 additional minutes.

Meanwhile, prepare the poached eggs. In a saucepan over high heat, bring 2 quarts of water and the salt to just under a boil, 180°F to 190°F. Lower the heat to a gentle simmer. Stir in the vinegar.

Set a fine-mesh sieve over a bowl. Working in batches, break an egg into the sieve to allow the thinner, excess whites to drain and discard. Carefully transfer each egg to an individual small bowl.

CONTINUED

Spicy Sweet Potato and Ham Hash with Spanish-Style Aioli

2 long red chile peppers, seeded and finely diced (or use 1 for less heat)

2 teaspoons chopped flat-leaf parsley, for garnish

½ teaspoon lime zest, for garnish

¼ teaspoon kosher salt

Pinch of freshly ground black pepper

Poached Eggs

1½ tablespoons kosher salt

1 tablespoon white wine vinegar

2 fresh eggs

Gently stir the water with a wooden spoon in a circular clockwise motion to create a whirlpool. Getting as close to the water as safely possible, carefully and swiftly tip the egg into the center of the whirlpool. Cook the egg until the whites are just set but the yolk is still soft, 3 to 5 minutes. Remove the egg with a slotted spoon and rest the spoon with the egg on a clean towel momentarily to drain excess water. Repeat this step with the remaining egg. (To make ahead, place the poached egg in an ice bath and refrigerate up to 8 hours. Reheat in warm water just before serving.)

Set the oven rack about 4 inches from the heat source and preheat the broiler.

Add the cooked ham and chile peppers to the skillet of potatoes, tossing to combine, then transfer to the oven for 2 to 3 minutes to crisp up. Carefully remove the skillet from the oven and divide the hash into two wide, shallow bowls. Drizzle with the aioli. Top each dish with a poached egg and sprinkle with the parsley and lime zest. Season with the salt and pepper.

Prep Time: 20 minutes, plus
1 hour chilling time
Cook Time: 45 minutes

Crepes with Brown Butter Bourbon Apples and Lemon Sauce

This recipe is inspired by "Apple Pan Dore," a most delicate and rich breakfast I once enjoyed at Mama's On Washington Square in San Francisco. It was a thinly sliced baguette (cut lengthwise) made into a light golden French toast, topped with warm, thinly sliced apples and drizzled with a lemon butter sauce. I had to try re-creating this dish at home, starting with the crisp apples and tangy lemon-vanilla sauce. I ultimately decided to complement the apples with another favorite French breakfast treat—the crepe! I suggest you reserve this breakfast for a special occasion or lazy Sunday brunch to be lingered over with a mimosa or latte. The crepes, apples, and sauce can be prepared individually, then warmed and assembled right before serving.

Batter

1¼ cups all-purpose flour

2 eggs

1½ tablespoons melted unsalted butter, plus more for brushing on the pan

2 teaspoons granulated sugar

1 teaspoon vanilla bean paste or vanilla extract

1⅓ cups milk

Sauce

½ cup water

⅓ cup granulated sugar

3 tablespoons fresh lemon juice

1 tablespoon cornstarch

½ teaspoon vanilla bean paste or vanilla extract

¼ teaspoon lemon zest

2 tablespoons unsalted butter, at room temperature

To make the batter: In a large bowl or blender, add the flour, eggs, melted butter, granulated sugar, and vanilla bean paste and whisk or blend until thoroughly combined. Gradually pour in the milk and whisk or blend until smooth. Cover and refrigerate for at least 1 hour.

To make the sauce: In a small saucepan over medium heat, whisk to combine the water, granulated sugar, lemon juice, cornstarch, vanilla bean paste, and lemon zest. Bring to a boil. Lower the heat and simmer for about 3 minutes, stirring occasionally, until the sauce has thickened. Remove from the heat and stir in the butter until the sauce is completely smooth. Cover and keep warm until ready to serve. (If making ahead, store in an airtight container for up to 5 days. If the sauce has become too thick, add a teaspoon of water at a time until the desired consistency is reached.)

To make the filling: Peel and cut the apples into ¼-inch-thick slices and transfer to a bowl. Add the lemon juice and gently toss to coat. In a large sauté pan over medium heat, add the butter and cook while stirring until brown flecks appear and the butter has a nutty aroma, about 5 minutes. Add the apples and continue to cook while stirring until the apples just begin to soften, about 2 minutes. Stir in the granulated sugar, bourbon, vanilla, and salt and continue to cook for an additional 3 to 5 minutes, until the apples have caramelized and the liquid begins to thicken. (The apples should be soft, but not mushy.) Set aside.

CONTINUED

Crepes with Brown Butter Bourbon Apples and Lemon Sauce

Filling

2 Gala apples

2 teaspoons fresh lemon juice

3 tablespoons unsalted butter

3 tablespoons granulated sugar

1 tablespoon bourbon

1 teaspoon vanilla extract

Pinch of salt

1 tablespoon confectioners' sugar, sifted (optional)

To make the crepes: Preheat the oven to 200°F. Line a baking sheet with parchment paper.

Place a 10-inch crepe pan or nonstick skillet over medium heat for about 1 minute until hot. Lightly brush or coat the pan with some of the melted butter. Lift the pan up just above the heat and pour about ⅓ cup of the crepe batter while tilting the pan to thinly and evenly distribute the batter. Cook until the center is set and the edges begin to appear golden brown and slightly crisp, about 2 minutes. Using a spatula, gently flip the crepe over and cook for an additional 1 to 2 minutes, until golden. Transfer the cooked crepe to the baking sheet, cover loosely with aluminum foil, and place in the oven to keep warm. Repeat this process, occasionally wiping the pan clean with a paper towel, until all of the crepe batter has been used up.

To assemble the crepes, place a single layer of apple slices in the center of each crepe and fold the sides toward the middle. Sprinkle lightly with the confectioners' sugar, if using, and drizzle with the lemon sauce. Serve warm.

Cook's Note: Usually the first crepe will be a "test crepe" to see if the pan temperature needs adjustment. If your pan is not hot enough, the batter doesn't stick to the pan. If it's too hot, the batter will stick too quickly.

Prep Time: 25 minutes
Cook Time: 45 minutes

Waffles with Caramelized Bananas and Sticky Toffee Sauce

A golden brown waffle with a crisp shell and a light, fluffy interior—that's what weekend dreams are made of. These waffles use a little rice flour for extra crispiness. The waffle batter itself is not overly sweet, as the waffles are paired with caramelized bananas, a rich toffee sauce, and whipped brown butter. You can also use your favorite toppings—I love fresh berries and warm maple syrup—or swap out the bananas and caramelize slices of grapefruit or Cara Cara oranges, peels and pith removed.

Whipped Brown Butter

6 tablespoons brown butter (see page 196), at room temperature

1 tablespoon whole milk

Waffles

1¼ cups all-purpose flour

¼ cup white rice flour

2 teaspoons baking powder

½ teaspoon salt

3 eggs, separated

2 to 3 tablespoons granulated sugar

1½ cups whole milk

4 tablespoons unsalted butter, melted and cooled slightly

1 teaspoon vanilla extract

Caramelized Bananas

4 tablespoons unsalted butter

½ cup firmly packed brown sugar (or demerara sugar)

2 small ripe yet firm bananas, peeled and halved lengthwise

To make the whipped brown butter: In a stand mixer fitted with the whisk attachment, mix the brown butter and whole milk on low speed until combined, then increase the speed to high and mix until light and fluffy, about 3 minutes. Set aside until ready to use.

To make the waffles: Preheat an electric waffle iron to low or medium-low. Preheat the oven to 200°F. Place a wire rack on top of a baking sheet.

In a large bowl, whisk together the flour, rice flour, baking powder, and salt.

In the large bowl of a stand mixer fitted with the whisk attachment, beat the egg whites on medium-high until soft peak just begin to form, 1 to 2 minutes. Add the granulated sugar and continue to beat until glossy, firm peaks form, about 2 minutes.

In a separate bowl mix together the egg yolks, milk, butter, and vanilla. Stir until well blended.

Add the milk mixture to the dry ingredients while stirring until just incorporated and no dry flour is visible (some lumps in the batter are okay). Stir in about one-third of the egg whites to lighten the batter, then fold in the remaining egg whites until just incorporated with no white streaks remaining.

Using a ladle, pour about ½ cup of the batter into the center of the waffle iron (the amount of the batter will depend on your waffle iron). The waffles will take 3 to 5 minutes to bake and are usually done when the amount of steam coming out of the waffle iron slows down or your waffle iron indicates they are done.

CONTINUED

Waffles with Caramelized Bananas and Sticky Toffee Sauce

Toffee Sauce

2 tablespoons bourbon

½ teaspoon vanilla extract

¼ cup heavy cream

Pinch of salt

Cook's Note: Caramelized bananas are best enjoyed right away, but if you do find yourself with leftovers, you could bake them into a banana bread by laying them on top of the batter in the loaf pan right before baking, pushing them in slightly with your fingers.

Serve immediately or place the waffles in a single layer on the wire rack loosely covered with aluminum foil to keep warm in the oven until ready to serve.

To make the caramelized bananas: In a sauté pan over medium heat, add the butter and cook until melted. Add the brown sugar and stir until the sugar dissolves and the mixture starts to bubble, about 2 minutes. Add the bananas to the pan, flat side down, and cook until browned and caramelized, about 4 minutes. Tilt the pan to slow down the browning if needed. Using a large spatula, carefully transfer the bananas to a plate, flat side up, and set aside.

To make the toffee sauce: Remove the pan from the heat, add the bourbon and vanilla, and swirl the pan to blend. Add the cream and salt, stirring until evenly combined. (If making ahead, store in an airtight container up to 2 weeks. Gently reheat to warm before serving.)

Serve the waffles right away with the caramelized bananas, warm toffee sauce, and whipped brown butter.

Store any leftover waffles, completely cooled, in an airtight container in the freezer for up to 1 week. To reheat, place on a baking sheet, loosely covered with foil, and bake in a 350°F oven for 3 to 5 minutes, until crisp and warmed.

Pain Perdu with Apricot Syrup

MAKES 2 SERVINGS

Prep Time: 10 minutes,
plus a minimum of 2 hours
chilling time
Cook Time: 50 minutes

Mile-high slices of French toast from a loaf of country bread make a fantastically decadent brunch that's both crunchy on the outside and custardy on the inside. This fancy French toast will definitely count as both breakfast and lunch and could possibly be your dessert for the day, too, but it's more than worth it. If you're lucky to get your hands on some perfectly ripe Fuyu persimmons, they would be a fantastic substitute for the apricots.

Vanilla Bean Whipped Cream (optional)

½ cup cold heavy cream

1 to 2 teaspoons confectioners' sugar

1 teaspoon vanilla bean paste or vanilla extract

Toasted Almonds (optional)

1 tablespoon salted butter

¼ cup sliced raw almonds

Pinch of kosher salt

Pain Perdu

2 slices stale rustic country bread, 2 inches thick

1 cup whole milk

1 cup heavy cream

3 tablespoons granulated sugar

1 tablespoon amaretto

1 teaspoon vanilla bean paste or vanilla extract

Pinch of salt

3 eggs plus 4 egg yolks

1½ tablespoons salted butter

Almond flour, for dusting

Sugar, preferably demerara, for sprinkling

To make the vanilla bean whipped cream: Place your stand mixer bowl and whisk attachment in the freezer for at least 15 minutes to chill. Then, in the stand mixer fitted with the whisk attachment, beat the cream on medium-high for 1 minute. Decrease the speed to low, add the confectioners' sugar and vanilla bean paste, and return to medium-high speed. Mix for another 30 seconds or until the cream forms soft peaks, scraping the bottom and sides of the bowl as needed. Refrigerate for up to 2 hours before serving.

To make the toasted almonds: In a cast-iron skillet over medium heat, melt the butter. Add the almonds and salt and cook while stirring until lightly toasted. Remove from the pan and set aside to cool.

To make the pain perdu: Place the bread slices in a 9 by 13-inch baking pan or dish.

In a saucepan over low heat, add the milk, cream, granulated sugar, amaretto, vanilla bean paste, and salt. Stir until the sugar dissolves and the mixture is slightly warm, just below scalding. Remove from the heat.

In a large bowl placed on a kitchen towel for stability, add the eggs and yolks and whisk to combine. While whisking, gradually add the warm milk mixture and whisk until combined. Strain the mixture through a fine-mesh sieve and pour over the bread slices in the baking pan. Cover with plastic wrap and refrigerate for at least 6 hours and up to overnight, flipping halfway through.

Preheat the oven to 325°F.

Place a large cast-iron skillet over medium heat. Add the butter and let melt. Carefully remove the soaked bread from the custard, letting the excess liquid drip back into the baking pan. Sprinkle both sides of the soaked bread slices with a few pinches of almond flour and demerara sugar before placing them

CONTINUED

Pain Perdu with Apricot Syrup

Apricot Syrup

¾ cup water

¾ cup granulated sugar

1 tablespoon amaretto

3 apricots, pitted and cut into quarters

3 tablespoons unsalted butter

Pinch of flaky sea salt (optional)

in the skillet. Cook over medium heat until golden brown, 3 to 5 minutes, then flip and cook 3 to 5 minutes on the other side.

Transfer the bread to a wire rack set over a baking sheet and bake for 10 to 15 minutes, until slightly puffed in the center.

To make the apricot syrup: In a saucepan over medium heat, add the water, sugar, and amaretto and stir until the sugar has dissolved. Add the apricots and simmer over low heat for about 5 minutes, or until the apricots are tender. Strain the fruit and set aside, reserving the liquid in the pan. Simmer over medium-high heat, without stirring, for 5 to 10 minutes until it reduces and turns an amber color. Remove from the heat and stir in the butter and a pinch of flaky sea salt, if using, until smooth. Combine the apricots and syrup and serve warm. (If making ahead, store in an airtight container in the refrigerator for up to 3 days. Reheat the syrup with apricots over low heat. If needed, add a small amount of water, one dash at a time, until the desired consistency is reached.)

Place the warm pain perdu slices on plates. Use a slotted spoon to place the apricots on top of the pain perdu, then drizzle with the syrup. Finish with a dollop of vanilla bean whipped cream and a sprinkle of toasted almonds, if using.

Cook's Notes: Bread that has gone stale (hence the pain perdu translation, "lost bread") works best for this recipe. If you absolutely need to make this recipe on a day you do not have day-old or stale bread, you can fake it by baking fresh slices in the oven at 200°F for 5 to 10 minutes, until dry but not toasted. Your delicious fresh country loaf will initially be offended by this gesture but will eventually understand the pain was worth it for the end result.

If you have leftover liquid after soaking your bread, store it in an airtight container in the refrigerator for up to 3 days and use it to make a quick French toast later in the week. Or make a baked custard: Pour the leftover liquid into ramekins, place them in a hot-water bath, and bake in a 350°F oven until set, about 40 minutes.

Prep Time: 10 minutes,
plus a minimum of 2 hours
chilling time
Cook Time: 1 hour, plus
10 minutes cooling time

Overnight French Toast Casserole with Berries

We often turn to this recipe when kicking off a weekend spent with friends and family. The genius of it is that you can prepare it the night before, so in the morning most of your work is done and you can really spend time with your guests.

1 pound challah bread loaf, cut into 1-inch cubes

3 tablespoons salted butter, softened

8 ounces cream cheese

¼ cup sour cream or Greek yogurt

2 cups half-and-half, at room temperature

12 eggs

⅓ cup plus 1 tablespoon granulated sugar

⅓ cup firmly packed brown sugar

1 tablespoon bourbon

1 tablespoon vanilla extract

¼ teaspoon kosher salt

½ teaspoon nutmeg

½ teaspoon orange zest

½ pint blackberries

½ pint blueberries

Confectioners' sugar, for serving

Maple syrup, for serving

Cook's Note: If your loaf of challah bread is already stale, you can skip the toasting step. You want the bread to be dry so it will soak up the liquid as much as possible without getting soggy.

Preheat the oven to 325°F. Spread the bread cubes out onto an ungreased baking sheet and bake for 5 to 10 minutes, until dry and slightly toasted but not browned (see Cook's Note).

Grease a 9 by 13-inch baking pan with 1 tablespoon of butter; set aside.

Add the cream cheese and sour cream to a microwave-safe bowl, and heat in the microwave at 10 second intervals, stirring in between, for a total of 30 to 40 seconds, until softened and spreadable but not melted.

In a large bowl, whisk to combine the cream cheese mixture with the half-and-half (small bits of cream cheese remaining are okay). Add the eggs, ⅓ cup granulated sugar, brown sugar, bourbon, vanilla, salt, nutmeg, and orange zest and whisk until just combined.

Layer half of the toasted bread cubes in the prepared baking pan. Top with half of the blackberries and blueberries. Pour half of the egg mixture over bread. Repeat with remaining half of bread cubes, fruit, and egg mixture. Make sure all of the pieces of bread are soaked with the egg mixture, pushing down gently on any dry spots if necessary.

Cover the baking pan with plastic wrap and refrigerate for at least 2 hours or up to 1 day.

Preheat the oven to 350°F.

Remove the plastic wrap and dot the top of the casserole with the remaining 2 tablespoons of butter and sprinkle with the remaining tablespoon of granulated sugar. Cover with aluminum foil and bake for about 45 minutes, until puffed, golden brown, and mostly set in the center. If a crunchier top is desired, remove the foil for the final 5 to 10 minutes of baking. Let stand for 5 to 10 minutes before serving.

Dust with confectioners' sugar and serve with maple syrup.

Tomato Curry Baked Eggs

"Eggs in purgatory" or shakshuka is everywhere. Who doesn't love eggs baked in an herby and spicy tomato sauce? This recipe starts with an Indian-style tomato sauce that has subtle heat from the chile but is softened by the creamy coconut milk. Naan is obviously the perfect tool for cleaning the plate. If you have a full set of small baking dishes or large ramekins, this recipe could easily be scaled up for a larger crowd as an easy-to-serve brunch item.

2 tablespoons salted butter

½ small onion, diced

1 tablespoon peeled, finely grated fresh ginger

1 small garlic clove, minced

1 teaspoon minced fresh chile (like jalapeño), or ¼ teaspoon red pepper flakes

¼ teaspoon kosher salt, plus more as needed

Pinch of freshly ground black pepper, plus more as needed

2 teaspoons garam masala

½ teaspoon curry powder

½ teaspoon ground turmeric

1 can (14½-ounce) whole peeled tomatoes

½ teaspoon freshly squeezed lime juice

3 tablespoons chopped cilantro, plus more for garnish

2 tablespoons coconut milk

1 teaspoon granulated sugar

2 eggs

2 pieces fresh naan, warmed in the oven for serving

In a Dutch oven or heavy skillet over medium heat, warm the butter until sizzling. Add the onion, ginger, garlic, chile, salt, and pepper. Cook, stirring, until softened, about 5 minutes. Stir in the garam masala, curry powder, and turmeric, and cook until fragrant, about 1 minute. Add the tomatoes and lime juice, and continue to cook while crushing the tomatoes with a potato masher or wooden spoon until the tomatoes start to release juices, about 3 minutes. Add the cilantro, coconut milk, and sugar, and cook while stirring until the sauce starts to boil. Lower the heat to medium-low and gently simmer, stirring occasionally, for about 20 minutes or until thickened.

Preheat the oven to 375°F.

Transfer the sauce to two small baking dishes. Use the back of a spoon to make a well in the sauce. Crack 1 egg into each well, then season with additional salt and pepper to taste.

Bake until the sauce is bubbling and the egg whites are opaque but still slightly jiggly, 6 to 8 minutes.

Sprinkle with additional cilantro and serve right away with the naan for dipping.

Cook's Note: You can get a jump start on this recipe by making the sauce component of the dish (before adding eggs) ahead. Let the sauce cool before transferring it to an airtight container and store in the refrigerator for up to 3 days. Gently reheat until warm before proceeding.

Prep Time: 25 minutes, plus
2 hours bringing dough to
room temperature
Cook Time: 25 minutes

Breakfast Pizza with Crab

This recipe is like crab eggs Benedict meets breakfast pizza. Individual pizzas make a nice nest for a fried egg, and the egg doesn't need to be shared. (It's that "I like you but I'm not sharing this fried egg with you" kind of love.) It is a little tricky getting the egg to fry directly on the pizza; it will work best if you give it a head start in a nonstick skillet. Once the edges have set, carefully transfer it onto the center of the cooked pizza with only 1 to 2 minutes cook time remaining.

Homemade Pizza Dough (page 42); or 1 pound store-bought, divided into 2 pieces

8 ounces fresh lump crabmeat

1 tablespoon fresh lemon juice

2 teaspoons finely chopped fresh chives

1 teaspoon Old Bay seasoning

Dash of hot sauce, plus more for serving

1½ tablespoons salted butter

1 tablespoon all-purpose flour, plus more for dusting the peel

½ cup whole milk

1½ tablespoons heavy cream

1 bay leaf

¼ teaspoon dry mustard

¼ teaspoon kosher salt

Pinch of freshly ground black pepper

Semolina flour, for dusting the peel

¼ cup shredded Monterey Jack cheese

2 teaspoons olive oil

2 eggs

At least 2 hours before ready to shape the pizzas, remove the two balls of dough from the refrigerator. Let the dough come to room temperature in its container, about 2 hours.

See the instructions for making and shaping the pizza dough on page 42, including preheating the oven with the pizza stone.

In a bowl, add the crab, lemon juice, 1 teaspoon of the chives, Old Bay, and hot sauce, and gently toss to combine. Cover and refrigerate until ready to use.

To make the béchamel, in a small saucepan over medium heat, melt 1 tablespoon of the butter. Add the flour and cook, whisking constantly, for about 2 minutes. Gradually add in the in the milk and heavy cream, whisking until smooth. Continue to cook, stirring occasionally, until thickened. Add the bay leaf, dry mustard, salt, and pepper and stir until evenly incorporated. Set aside. Remove the bay leaf before using.

Rub a small amount of flour on the top of the pizza peel, then dust very lightly with semolina flour.

Using flat hands, gently transfer the shaped dough to the pizza peel, stretch and shape once again to the desired size and shape. Before adding toppings, gently move the pizza peel back and forth to test that the dough can slide easily without sticking. If the dough sticks, lift the dough and add a bit more semolina flour to the pizza peel and try again.

Spread the béchamel over the two pizzas, leaving a 1-inch border around the edges. Sprinkle with the cheese and add small dollops of the crab mixture. Lightly brush the edge of the pizzas with the olive oil.

Using the pizza peel (see Cook's Note), slide the pizza dough onto the baking stone in the oven. Bake for 6 to 8 minutes.

Meanwhile, in a nonstick skillet over medium heat, melt the remaining 1½ teaspoons of butter. Crack and gently add the eggs, side by side, and cook until the edges start to set, 2 to 3 minutes. Remove the pizzas from the oven and transfer one egg to the center of each pizza. Quickly return the pizzas to the oven and cook until the whites of the eggs are set but the yolks are slightly runny, 1 to 2 minutes. Remove from the oven by sliding the peel under the pizzas.

Let cool for 2 minutes. Garnish the pizzas with the remaining 1 teaspoon of chives and a dash of hot sauce. Leave each pizza whole and serve immediately.

Cook's Notes: Here's how to pizza peel like a pro: Once you have added pizza toppings, give the pizza peel another quick back-and-forth shake to make sure the dough is not sticking to the peel. Open the oven door, insert the peel, and tilt slightly to touch the peel toward the back of the baking stone. Give the peel a slight jerk to release the center edge of dough onto the back center of the stone, then gently shuffle the pizza as you slowly pull the peel away to land the pizza on the center of the stone.

If you don't have a pizza peel, you can use a rimless baking sheet typically used for cookies.

Prep Time: 5 hours (or 24 to
48 hours, if making ahead),
including inactive time
Cook Time: 10 minutes

Homemade Pizza Dough

My mother and I tested, baked, and adjusted all of the variables until we came up with a pizza dough we were excited about. To start, the very fine texture of the Italian-style or "00" flour produces a versatile, manageable dough, and with a protein content similar to that of bread flour, you can achieve more chewiness. Our criteria included a dough that could be kneaded by hand, a light airy interior, a crisp browned (but not burnt) crust, and a little chew to the bite. Many pizzas later, we came up with a dough recipe that we love.

The 24 to 48 hour "make-ahead" process for this pizza dough is a preferable method because it produces a more flavorful dough with great texture. However, if you don't have the time, I've laid out a couple extra steps that enable you to enjoy pizza the same day you make the dough.

¾ cup (180 grams) warm water (105°F to 110°F)

½ teaspoon (2 grams) active dry yeast

1 teaspoon (4 grams) granulated sugar

2¼ cups (270 grams) 00 flour, plus more for dusting

1 teaspoon (6 grams) kosher salt

1½ teaspoons (6 grams) olive oil, plus 1 teaspoon for oiling

Semolina flour (or cornmeal flour), for dusting

Add the warm water to a bowl, then add the yeast and sugar and stir until just combined. Set aside for 10 to 15 minutes, until it appears cloudy with a little foam.

In a separate bowl, whisk together the flour and salt. Gradually add the flour mixture to the yeast mixture while stirring with a fork, and mix until the dough comes together into a soft, shaggy mass, about 1 minute. (If the dough is very dry and stiff, add water in ½-teaspoon increments. If excessively wet, dust with flour in small increments, but err on the side of a soft, wet dough.) Add 1½ teaspoons of the oil and knead in the bowl with your hands until just incorporated, about 1 minute.

On a clean work surface, using lightly oiled or wet hands (to help prevent sticking), knead the dough for 3 minutes. To knead the dough, stretch the dough by pushing the center of the dough forward with the palms of your hands until it resists slightly. Fold the dough in half onto itself, starting at the end of the dough furthest from you, lifting the ends of the dough up and pulling down over the bottom half of the dough. Turn the dough by rotating it 90 degrees. Repeat. Let the dough rest for 15 minutes.

Knead the dough by hand again for an additional 3 minutes until dough is satiny smooth and soft.

If you are making two individual pizzas, use a sharp knife or a bench cutter to cut the dough in half and follow the steps for each ball of dough separately.

Form the dough into a ball, holding the dough in both hands and using your fingers to stretch the ends of the dough down and tucking them underneath itself, continuing to do so until you form a ball of dough with a smooth, taut surface on top. Gather and pinch the bottom ends until you have a tightly sealed seam.

Transfer the dough, seam side down, to a lightly oiled bowl covered tightly with plastic wrap and store in the refrigerator for 24 to 48 hours. About 2 hours before ready to shape dough, remove the dough from the refrigerator and let rest until it comes to room temperature.

If preparing the dough to bake the pizza the same day, knead one time according to the directions above. Instead of forming the dough into a ball, transfer to a lightly oiled bowl and cover with a clean, damp kitchen towel or plastic wrap. Let sit at room temperature until doubled in size, about 1½ hours. Deflate the dough by gently patting into a square. Pull each of the corners towards the center of the dough then flip the dough over so the smooth side is facing up. Form the dough into a ball according to the directions above. Return the dough to the bowl, cover with a towel, and allow to rest in a warm, dry place for 1½ to 2 hours.

At least 30 to 45 minutes before baking, set the oven rack to the bottom-most shelf of the oven, and set the baking stone on the rack. Preheat the oven to 550°F (or 500°F, depending on the highest temperature your oven allows).

While the oven and baking stone are preheating, prepare the pizza toppings and have them ready to use.

Once the pizza dough is at room temperature (if following the 24 hour directions) or after the dough has had its second rise (if following the same day directions) it's time to shape the dough.

To shape the dough: On a lightly floured surface, gently press the ball of dough with the tips of your fingers starting in the center and working outward to about ½ inch from the border of the dough circle. (This helps remove any large air bubbles and begins to gradually stretch and shape the dough. Do not roll the dough.) Gently lift the dough about ½ inch in from the border and continue to gently stretch the dough while lifting and rotating, until the desired size is achieved (6 to 8 inches in diameter for two individual pizzas or 12 to 14 inches for a single pizza).

Rub a small amount of flour on the top of the pizza peel, then dust lightly with semolina flour.

Using flat hands, gently transfer the shaped dough to the pizza peel, gently re-shaping to the desired size if needed. Before adding toppings, gently move the pizza peel back and forth to test that the dough can slide easily without sticking. If the dough sticks, lift the dough and add a bit more semolina flour to the pizza peel and try again. (See page 41 for more tips about using a pizza peel.)

Add the desired toppings and bake as directed in Breakfast Pizza with Crab (page 40) or Pizza with Caramelized Figs, Baby Arugula, and Smoked Mozzarella (page 145).

Cook's Notes: The slow rise (24 to 48 hours after the second kneading) produces a bit more flavorful dough with great texture and seemed effortless. The same day method also produced a delicious dough; if you are home and want pizza the same day, it is a great option.

Black Pepper Biscuits with Cauliflower Gravy

I have always had some part of me that wants to be Southern. I don't know where it comes from, but it has always been there. I even named my dog Georgia. I finally got to visit Savannah after years of romanticizing their historic homes with porches and live oak draped with Spanish moss. It was as magical as I imagined it to be, and I'm even more smitten. These biscuits and gravy are a riff on the Southern classic. The creamy white gravy is made with oven-roasted and pureed cauliflower. Just the notion of such a thing would be sure to highly offend a true Southerner. And I just love that about them.

To pull together this comforting breakfast a little more quickly, you can make the gravy in advance and just reheat it while the biscuits are baking.

Gravy

½ head cauliflower, finely chopped

1 small onion, cut into quarters

1 garlic clove

2 tablespoons olive oil

¼ teaspoon salt

¼ cup water

1½ to 2 cups milk

1½ tablespoons duck fat or bacon grease

2 tablespoons all-purpose flour

¼ teaspoon finely chopped thyme

¼ teaspoon kosher salt

To make the gravy: Preheat the oven to 475°F.

On a baking sheet, toss together the cauliflower, onion, garlic, olive oil, salt, and pepper. Roast for about 20 minutes, or until the cauliflower is fork-tender and starting to brown. Set aside to let cool slightly, then add to a food processor and puree with the water until very smooth. If mixture is too thick to blend, add up to ½ cup of the milk. Set aside.

In a large skillet over medium-low heat, melt the duck fat. Add the flour, stirring constantly, and cook for 3 to 5 minutes until starting to turn a light golden brown. Gradually add in 1½ cups of the milk and continue to cook, while whisking, until smooth, thickened, and starting to bubble. Add in the cauliflower puree and stir to combine. Season with the thyme and salt. Turn the heat down to low and simmer for a few minutes, stirring occasionally, until smooth and uniform. Serve hot. (If making ahead, store the gravy in an airtight container in the refrigerator for up to 3 days. Reheat over low heat, adding a few tablespoons of water if needed to achieve the desired consistency.)

To make the biscuits: Preheat the oven to 425°F. Line a baking sheet with parchment paper.

In a large mixing bowl, whisk to combine the flour, sugar, baking powder, baking soda, salt, and ½ teaspoon of the pepper. Toss the butter into the flour mixture and cut it in with a pastry blender or two knives until the butter is just coated in flour and is in pea-size pieces. Make a well in the flour mixture.

Biscuits

1⅓ cups (160 grams) all-purpose flour, plus more for dusting

2 teaspoons granulated sugar

2 teaspoons baking powder

¼ teaspoon baking soda

½ teaspoon salt

½ teaspoon freshly ground black pepper, plus more for sprinkling tops before baking

4 tablespoons cold unsalted butter, cut into small cubes

⅓ cup cold buttermilk, plus more if dough appears dry

⅓ cup cold sour cream

1½ tablespoons cold heavy cream

Whisk the buttermilk and sour cream together until blended. Pour the buttermilk mixture into the flour well and mix with a fork until just incorporated. If the mixture appears dry, add additional buttermilk in tablespoon increments until the dough looks wet.

Turn the dough onto a lightly floured wood board. Using flour-coated hands, gently gather and pat the dough into a 6-inch square, approximately 1 inch thick. Dip a 3-inch round cutter into flour, then press straight down into the dough to cut out biscuits. Arrange the biscuits on the baking sheet so that the sides of the biscuits touch. Brush the biscuit tops with the heavy cream and sprinkle with the remaining ¼ teaspoon pepper. Bake for 15 to 20 minutes, rotating the baking sheet halfway through, until the biscuits are golden brown on top. Serve warm with the gravy for dipping.

Cook's Note: Handle the dough gently and as little as possible for tender, flaky biscuits.

Prep Time: 30 minutes, plus
20 minutes chilling time
Cook Time: 1 hour, plus
15 minutes cooling time

Black Cherry Crumb Cake

This is a New York–style crumb cake, with a generous crumb layer that reminds me of when a Long Island kid like me got to roll into the deli and pick out a Yoo-hoo from the cooler and a block of mile-high crumb cake wrapped in plastic wrap. I'm not sure if those kind of days are gone, but I'm trying to bring them back with this recipe, and adding some fruit to help it blend in with the healthier choices of today's generation. Dark sweet cherries are incorporated both in the batter and in a jam that is swirled through the top of the batter, hiding right under the crumbs.

Crumb Topping

¾ cup firmly packed brown sugar

½ cup granulated sugar

½ cup (4 ounces) unsalted butter, melted and cooled slightly

½ teaspoon freshly grated nutmeg

¼ teaspoon kosher salt

1¼ cups (150 grams) all-purpose flour

Compote

¾ cup fresh or frozen dark sweet cherries, pitted

2 tablespoons granulated sugar

1 tablespoon brandy (or kirsch)

Cake

1½ cups plus 2 tablespoons (195 grams) all-purpose flour

½ cup plus 2 tablespoons granulated sugar

2 tablespoons cornstarch

1 teaspoon baking powder

½ teaspoon baking soda

½ teaspoon kosher salt

To make the crumb topping: Whisk together both sugars, the melted butter, nutmeg, and salt in a bowl. Add in the flour and mix with a fork until it comes together into clumps. Cover and place in the freezer to cool and harden, about 20 minutes.

To make the compote: In a small saucepan, combine the cherries, granulated sugar, and brandy. Bring to a boil, then turn down the heat to medium-low and cook, stirring frequently, until the fruit has softened and the juices begin to thicken, about 15 minutes. Set aside to cool.

To make the cake: Preheat the oven to 325°F. Lightly grease an 8-inch square baking pan with butter.

In a stand mixer fitted with the whisk attachment, add the flour, granulated sugar, cornstarch, baking powder, baking soda, and salt and mix on low until evenly combined.

Change to the paddle attachment and, with the mixer at medium-low speed, add the butter, a tablespoon at a time. Beat for 1 to 2 minutes, until the mixture resembles evenly coarse sand.

In a separate bowl, whisk together the buttermilk, egg and egg yolk, and vanilla.

With the mixer on low speed, pour the egg mixture into the flour mixture and blend until just incorporated, then increase the speed to medium-high and beat until light and fluffy, 1 to 2 minutes, scraping the sides and bottom of the bowl as needed.

Pour the batter into the prepared baking pan. Smooth and level the surface with an offset spatula. Top evenly with the cooled compote, then gently

CONTINUED

CONTINUED

Black Cherry Crumb Cake

6 tablespoons unsalted butter

¾ cup buttermilk (or sour cream)

1 egg plus 1 egg yolk, at room temperature

1 teaspoon vanilla extract

¾ cup fresh or frozen dark sweet cherries, pitted

Confectioners' sugar, for dusting

swirl the batter and compote together with a knife or chopstick, leaving behind visible streaks of jam.

Top with an even layer of the cherries, pressing them slightly into the batter.

Break the crumb topping into crumbs, leaving some larger chunks intact, and gently sprinkle them over the batter until evenly and completely covered.

Bake for about 45 minutes, or until the edges are golden brown and a cake tester inserted into the center comes out clean. Let cool in the pan on a wire rack for 15 to 20 minutes, then remove from the pan. Dust with confectioners' sugar before cutting into squares and serving.

If making ahead, cover tightly with plastic wrap or store in an airtight container in a cool, dry place for up to 2 days or in the freezer for up to 1 month. Let thaw at room temperature in the sealed container.

Cardamom Cinnamon Rolls with Coffee Icing

This recipe is a little bit of an activity, ideal for getting the dough started on a snowy or rainy day. Better yet, start the night before the storm so you can enjoy them in the morning with minimal effort. The slow overnight rise makes a superior bread in flavor and texture, and the cardamom-and-coffee flavor combo lends a delicate depth of flavor to this rich morning treat. Making a yeast-risen dough is an exciting and rewarding process in itself—to see ingredients come alive, literally, and to be the conductor of their final product is my idea of a good time. But even if you're not just in it for the sweet satisfaction of homemade dough, your efforts will be rewarded with soft and billowy brioche rolls and that amazing smell filling your kitchen. And let's not forget the pot of gold at the end of the rainbow—that super soft, gooey center of the roll.

Dough

½ cup whole milk, warmed to 110°F

1 package (2¼ teaspoons) active dry yeast

½ teaspoon granulated sugar plus 3 tablespoons

4 eggs plus 1 egg yolk

3½ cups (420 grams) bread flour (plus more for dusting and additional if the dough is excessively sticky)

1 teaspoon kosher salt

1 teaspoon ground cardamom

1 cup unsalted butter, at room temperature (butter should be cool, soft, and pliable; not oily or warm)

To make the dough: In a glass measuring cup, add the milk, yeast, and ½ teaspoon of the granulated sugar. Whisk until just combined. Let sit at room temperature until bubbly and almost doubled in volume with a domed top, 10 to 15 minutes. (This test ensures the yeast is alive and well before proceeding.) Add the eggs and egg yolk and whisk to combine.

In a stand mixer fitted with the paddle attachment, add the flour and slowly pour in the yeast and egg mixture with the mixer running on low speed until dry flour is no longer visible, 1 to 2 minutes. Cover with a clean kitchen towel and let the dough rest at room temperature for about 20 minutes.

Switch over to the dough hook. Add the remaining 3 tablespoons of sugar, salt, and cardamom and mix on medium-low until evenly distributed, about 1 minute. Scrape the bottom and sides of the bowl with a spatula and continue to mix on medium-low until the dough comes together in a smooth, cohesive mass, 3 to 5 minutes. With the mixer on, gradually add the butter, a tablespoon or two at a time, waiting until each addition of butter is incorporated into the dough before adding more. Continue until all of the butter has been added, occasionally scraping down the bowl and dough hook with a spatula. This process can take up to 15 minutes.

CONTINUED

Cardamom Cinnamon Rolls with Coffee Icing

Filling

½ cup firmly packed brown sugar

¼ cup granulated sugar

1 tablespoon ground cinnamon

¼ cup salted butter, at room temperature

2 egg whites, lightly beaten

Icing

3 tablespoons cream cheese, at room temperature

2 tablespoons salted butter, at room temperature

1⅓ cups confectioners' sugar

1¼ teaspoons espresso powder

1 teaspoon vanilla extract

Once all of the butter has been added, continue to mix until the dough is climbing the dough hook and barely sticking to the bottom of the bowl, about 10 minutes. The finished dough should be silky smooth, soft, and slightly springy. (If the dough is excessively sticky and wet, you can add 1 tablespoon flour at a time, up to ¼ cup.)

Shape into a ball and place in a lightly greased bowl, cover with plastic wrap, and let it rise at room temperature until nearly doubled in volume, about 1 hour.

To deflate the dough, turn the dough onto a clean, very lightly floured work surface. Pat the dough out into a rectangle, with the longer side closest to you, using your hands to press out air bubbles. Fold the dough into thirds, as if you are folding a business letter. Rotate the dough so the longest side is closest to you and repeat with a gentle pat and letter fold. You should be left with a thick square of dough with visible layers of folds. Tuck the corners under to round out the dough. Place the dough seam side down into the oiled bowl, cover tightly with plastic wrap, and refrigerate for at least 6 hours (or up to 12 hours). If the dough has more than doubled in volume within 1 or 2 hours of refrigeration, deflate the dough by repeating the pat and letter-fold technique. (Once the butter is sufficiently chilled, after 2 to 3 hours of refrigeration, it will prevent the dough from rising further.)

Line a 9 by 13-inch baking pan with parchment paper and set aside.

To make the filling: In a bowl, stir together the sugars, cinnamon, butter, and half of the beaten egg whites until well combined. Set aside.

Place the dough in the center of a large piece of parchment paper, and roll the dough into a rectangle that is uniformly ½ inch thick and approximately 12 by 18 inches, with the longer side of the rectangle closest to you. Use a spatula or the back of a spoon to gently spread the filling mixture over the rectangle, all the way to the edges.

Use flat hands to gently press the filling into the dough. Working from the long side, use the tips of your fingers to start to rolling the dough into a tight and even spiral. Move your fingers along the dough from the center and out to the edges as you roll to create a straight and even log. Once

Cook's Notes: To prepare the dough ahead of time, you can freeze the dough just before shaping and right after the second rise (either at room temperature or in the refrigerator). Deflate the dough, wrap it airtight with plastic wrap, and store it in the freezer for up to a month. Thaw the dough, still wrapped, in the refrigerator overnight and use it directly from the refrigerator.

the first spiral is started, you can use the heels of your hands to push and roll the dough. Pull the dough slightly at the seam edge to stretch and pinch to seal. With the roll seam side down, use a piece of unflavored, unwaxed dental floss (or a sharp knife) to cut 12 rolls, each measuring about 1½ inch thick. Place the rolls, cutside up, into the pan, evenly spaced, and cover with plastic wrap. Meanwhile, preheat the oven to 375°F.

Let the rolls sit at room temperature until nearly doubled in size, 30 to 45 minutes. When proofed and ready to bake, the dough should hold a slight indentation when pressed gently with a finger.

Before baking, remove the plastic wrap and brush the tops of the rolls lightly with the remaining egg white. Cover with nonstick aluminum foil and bake for about 25 minutes. Remove the foil and return to the oven to bake for an additional 10 to 20 minutes, or until golden brown on top and the center is mostly set. (The internal temperature should read 190°F to 195°F).

To make the icing: In a small bowl, combine the cream cheese, butter, confectioners' sugar, espresso powder, and vanilla until smooth and well incorporated.

Let the rolls cool for about 10 minutes before evenly distributing the icing on top of the rolls with an offset spatula or knife.

Bourbon Granola with White Chocolate and Apricots (or Good Graces Granola)

Making this granola is a monthly, or sometimes biweekly, ritual in our house. You can almost always find some in a hinged jar on the counter. It's such a treat to have some always at the ready to enjoy a quick and easy breakfast together before starting the day—just add some to a bowl of yogurt with fresh fruit. It's also become one of our favorite little gifts to package up and give to our friends. We once gave a bag to our doctor, who went crazy over it, and we joke that this granola has forever put us in her good graces.

2 cups thick rolled oats

½ cup unsweetened coconut flakes

¼ cup sliced raw almonds

¼ cup chopped raw hazelnuts

2 teaspoons chia seeds

3½ tablespoons unsalted butter

¼ cup firmly packed brown sugar

1 teaspoon vanilla extract

¼ teaspoon kosher salt

Pinch of ground cardamom

Pinch of ground cinnamon

1 tablespoon bourbon

1 egg white

¼ cup white chocolate chips

⅓ cup chopped, dried apricots

Preheat the oven to 325°F. Line a baking sheet with parchment paper.

In a large bowl, toss together the rolled oats, coconut, both nuts, and chia seeds.

In a small saucepan over low heat, add the butter, brown sugar, vanilla, salt, cardamom, and cinnamon. Stir until well combined and completely smooth. Increase the heat to medium and continue to cook until the mixture starts to simmer and bubble, about 3 minutes. Remove the pan from the heat, add the bourbon, and stir to combine.

In a separate bowl, whisk the egg white vigorously until frothy.

Pour the warm butter and sugar mixture over the oat mixture and stir until evenly coated. Fold in the egg white. Spread the mixture onto the baking sheet in an even layer and bake for about 25 minutes, stirring with a spatula after 15 minutes, until golden brown and dry to the touch. Remove from the oven and let cool slightly, about 5 minutes, before using a spatula to mix in the white chocolate chips and apricots. The white chocolate chips should melt slightly as you stir.

Let cool completely before transferring the granola to an airtight container, leaving some medium-size clusters intact. Store at room temperature for up to 2 weeks or for several weeks in the freezer.

Nourishing Tropical Kale Smoothie

My sister has been making some version of this smoothie (without a recipe) for years. It changes a little bit day to day and has even evolved over the years with changing tastes and diets in their household, but I coaxed a recipe out of her and translated "handfuls" and "big spoons" into measurements so I could try to preserve what I consider the original version. I first encountered it when she left it outside my door almost every morning of a particularly trying week I was having. Let this be your "starter smoothie" to give yourself a little boost in the morning, or make it for someone you love who you think might need a little help, too.

5 cups chopped kale, stems removed

1½ to 2 cups water

1 small banana, frozen

⅓ cup pineapple chunks, frozen

⅓ cup mango chunks, frozen

⅓ cup mixed berries, frozen

2 tablespoons plain yogurt

1 tablespoon coconut cream

1 tablespoon ground flaxseeds

1 teaspoon honey

1 tablespoon raw cashews (or 1 scoop plant-based protein powder; optional)

Unsweetened coconut flakes, for garnish (optional)

In a high-powered blender, add all of the ingredients and blend until smooth and creamy, about 1 minute. If desired, garnish with a few sprinkles of coconut flakes.

This is best served right away, but if making ahead, cover and store the smoothie toward the back of the refrigerator (or coldest area) overnight and stir well with a spoon to remix.

Lunch

(Soups, Salads & Sandwiches)

Roasted Heirloom Tomato Soup // 59

Three Little Pigs Split Pea Soup // 60

French Onion Soup // 63

Chicken Tortilla Soup with Lime Chipotle Crema // 64

Butter Lettuce with Citrus Vinaigrette // 67

Kale Salad with Daikon Radish and
Green Goddess Dressing // 68

Crab Louie Salad // 71

Little Gems with Watermelon Radish,
Crispy Prosciutto, and Humboldt Fog // 72

Classic Wedge Salad with Blue Cheese and Bacon // 75

Roasted Beet Salad with Arugula, Feta, and Edamame // 76

Charred Radicchio, Avocado, and Pear Salad with
Buttermilk Dressing // 79

Grilled Curry Chicken Salad Lettuce Cups // 80

Greek-Style Panzanella // 83

Soba Noodle Salad with Tofu and Charred
Green Onions // 84

Cucumber Sandwich with Harissa Yogurt // 87

Cold-Pressed Roasted Eggplant Sandwich with
Parsley Pistachio Pesto // 88

Grilled Cheese with Gruyère and Caramelized Onions // 91

Open-Faced Niçoise-Style Tuna Melt // 92

Bacon, Lettuce, and Tomato with Tomato Jam (BLTTJ) // 94

Sweet Italian Sausage and Pepper Sandwich // 95

French Dip Sandwich with Au Jus // 97

Prep Time: 15 minutes
Cook Time: 1 hour, plus
10 minutes cooling time

Roasted Heirloom Tomato Soup

If you are able to get your hands on some fresh heirloom tomatoes at a local market or farmers' market, it is reason to celebrate. I love each and every color, shape, and marvelously perfect imperfection. Heirlooms are bright, juicy, sweetly acidic, and elaborately flavorful. They deserve only the finest extra-virgin olive oil, freshest herbs, and roasting, which highlights and concentrates the natural flavors.

4 pounds heirloom tomatoes, cored and quartered

½ large onion, preferably Vidalia, cut into 8 wedges

4 garlic cloves

¼ cup extra-virgin olive oil

1½ teaspoons kosher salt

1 teaspoon freshly ground black pepper

2 to 2½ cups vegetable stock, depending on the desired thickness of the soup

2 tablespoons chopped flat-leaf parsley

2 tablespoons coarsely chopped basil

2 ounces shaved Parmesan cheese, preferably Parmigiano-Reggiano

Preheat the oven to 400°F. Line two baking sheets with parchment paper.

Arrange the tomatoes, onion, and garlic in a single layer on both baking sheets with the tomatoes toward the outside border and the garlic and onion in the center. Drizzle evenly with the olive oil and sprinkle with the salt and pepper.

Roast for 20 to 25 minutes, turning halfway through, until the tomatoes release juices and soften.

Transfer the roasted vegetables with juices to a large saucepan and add 2 cups of vegetable stock. Cook uncovered over medium heat until it comes to a boil. Turn the heat down to low and let simmer for about 30 minutes, or until the vegetables have softened and the liquid has reduced to about two-thirds of the original volume. Let cool slightly, about 10 minutes, before carefully transferring to a blender. Blend until smooth (or use an immersion blender and blend until smooth). Add up to ½ cup of the remaining vegetable stock if the soup seems too thick. If making ahead, let cool slightly then transfer to an airtight container and store in the refrigerator for up to 2 days. Rewarm before proceeding.

Return the soup to the saucepan over medium heat, add the parsley and 1 tablespoon of the basil, and stir to combine. Let simmer for 2 to 3 minutes until warm.

Ladle the soup into serving bowls and garnish with the remaining 1 tablespoon basil and the Parmesan.

Three Little Pigs Split Pea Soup

As the recipe name alludes, this split pea soup features a powerhouse trio of pork in its most comfort food–type forms. This hearty, down-home meal can provide warmth on even the coldest of days.

3 slices bacon, diced

4 ounces thick ham steak, diced

4 ounces hot smoked sausage (uncured), diced

1 large onion, preferably Vidalia, chopped

½ teaspoon kosher salt, plus more as needed

½ teaspoon freshly ground black pepper, plus more as needed

1½ cups peeled and chopped carrots

1½ cups chopped celery

4 cups chicken stock

4 cups water

2 bay leaves

¼ teaspoon finely chopped rosemary

¼ teaspoon finely chopped thyme

1 pound green split peas, rinsed and drained

2 Yukon gold potatoes, peeled and cut into ½-inch cubes

2 tablespoons chopped celery leaves

2 tablespoons chopped flat-leaf parsley

⅓ cup frozen peas

In a large stockpot over medium-high heat, sauté the bacon until beginning to brown but not crisp. Add the ham and sausage and cook for 3 to 4 minutes, stirring occasionally, until lightly browned. Transfer the meats to a plate and set aside, reserving the grease in the pot.

Add the onion to the pot and cook, stirring occasionally, until translucent, about 5 minutes. Season with the salt and pepper. Add the carrots and celery and cook, stirring occasionally, until beginning to soften, about 3 minutes. Return the meats to the pot and stir. Add the chicken stock, water, bay leaves, rosemary, and thyme and stir to combine. Add the split peas, stirring to combine, and bring to a simmer. Turn down the heat to low, cover the pot, and cook for 2 to 2½ hours.

Uncover, increase the heat, and cook until just beginning to boil. Add the potatoes, celery leaves, and parsley, stirring to combine. Turn down the heat and simmer uncovered for 10 minutes or until the potatoes are fork-tender. Turn off the heat and stir in the frozen peas. Remove and discard the bay leaves. Season to taste with additional salt and pepper and serve warm.

If making ahead, allow to cool, then store in an airtight container in the refrigerator for up to 5 days or in the freezer for up to 2 months. Let thaw overnight in the refrigerator before reheating until warm.

French Onion Soup

This soup calls for black garlic, which is garlic that has undergone something like a fermentation process to create a complex, mild, and sweet flavor and a soft texture. It can be found online, but I've also come across it at Trader Joe's and Whole Foods Market. It gives this classic soup a unique, but appropriate, depth of flavor that complements and enhances the real star of the show—the caramelized onions.

Soup

2 tablespoons salted butter

1 tablespoon olive oil

5 small yellow onions, thinly sliced

½ teaspoon kosher salt

¼ teaspoon freshly ground black pepper

1 small garlic clove, minced

2 black garlic cloves, minced

½ teaspoon chopped thyme

4 cups low-sodium beef stock

¼ cup dry red wine

2 teaspoons balsamic vinegar

3 ounces mozzarella, grated

3 ounces Gruyère, grated

Crostini

2 tablespoons extra-virgin olive oil

2 (1-inch) slices sourdough bread

Pinch of kosher salt

Pinch of freshly ground black pepper

To make the soup: In a Dutch oven or heavy skillet over medium-low heat, warm the butter and olive oil. Add the onions, sprinkle with the salt, and cook for about 15 minutes, stirring occasionally, until softened and translucent.

Add the pepper, garlic, black garlic, and thyme. Continue to cook on medium-low heat for an additional 20 to 30 minutes, stirring often, until the onions have turned mahogany brown and smell sweet.

Add the stock, wine, and vinegar. Bring to a boil, then turn down the heat to low, cover, and let simmer for 30 minutes. (If making ahead, let cool slightly then transfer to an airtight container and store in the refrigerator for up to 2 days. Rewarm before continuing.)

To make the crostini: Preheat the oven to 400°F. Use a pastry brush to coat both sides of the bread with the oil. Place the bread on a baking sheet and season with the salt and pepper. Bake for about 6 minutes, flipping with a spatula halfway through, until lightly toasted on both sides. Set aside until ready to use or let cool completely before storing in an airtight container at room temperature for up to 1 day.

Preheat the broiler.

Set a pair of oven-safe bowls on a baking sheet. Ladle the soup into the bowls, leaving about ½ inch of room in the bowl for the bread and cheese toppings. Arrange the crostini in a single layer on top of the soup, cutting the bread to fit if necessary. Sprinkle the crostini generously with both cheeses, letting a little hang over the edge of the bowl. Place the baking sheet in the oven and broil for about 5 minutes, checking frequently, until the cheese is brown and bubbly. Allow to cool slightly before serving.

Chicken Tortilla Soup with Lime Chipotle Crema

The combination of savory, spicy, bright, and creamy flavors in this soup will have you craving seconds and thinking of when you can make it again. The soup and crema can be prepared a day or two ahead—in fact, it's best that way to allow the flavor to develop fully. The mildly spicy kick is balanced by the avocado and crema, and the fresh lime and crispy tortillas are musts to round out the flavors and textures. The soup is best served surrounded by the extras so you can individualize it to your liking. On a personal note, this could be the first known cure for a "man cold"—with all the soothing comforts of warm chicken soup and a little kick of heat that says, "Buck up, buttercup" at the same time.

Tortilla Strips

3 corn tortillas

1 tablespoon canola oil

¼ teaspoon kosher salt

Pinch of cayenne pepper

Soup

1 teaspoon ground cumin

½ teaspoon garlic powder

½ teaspoon onion salt

¼ teaspoon cayenne pepper

1 onion, diced

1 orange or yellow bell pepper, seeded and diced

2 jalapeño peppers, seeded and finely diced

2 tablespoons olive oil

Juice and zest of 1 lime

½ teaspoon salt

To make the tortilla strips: Preheat the oven to 350°F. Generously brush both sides of the tortillas with oil and arrange them in a single layer on a baking sheet. Season with salt and cayenne. Bake for about 8 minutes, flipping halfway through, until crisp and lightly golden brown. Cut into strips right away as they will crisp up more while they cool.

To make the soup: Preheat the oven to 375°F with oven racks in the upper and lower thirds. Line a rimmed baking sheet with aluminum foil.

In a small bowl combine the cumin, garlic powder, onion salt, and cayenne. Set aside.

To the baking sheet, add the onion, bell pepper, and jalapeños. Drizzle with oil and lime juice and toss to coat. Sprinkle with salt and zest. Place the baking sheet on the upper rack of the oven and roast for about 20 minutes, or until the vegetables are softened and just starting to brown.

Pat the chicken thighs dry with paper towels and rub both sides with butter to coat. Sprinkle the thighs evenly with the cumin seasoning mixture and add them to a Dutch oven. Place the Dutch oven on the lower rack of the oven and roast, uncovered, for 20 minutes, flipping the thighs halfway through.

4 skinless bone-in chicken thighs

2 tablespoons salted butter, at room temperature

2 garlic cloves, minced

4 cups chicken stock

1 corn tortilla

Chipotle Crema

⅓ cup sour cream

2 tablespoons heavy cream

1 tablespoon fresh lime juice

¼ teaspoon chipotle powder

Pinch of salt

1 ripe avocado, cut into ¼-inch slices

2 tablespoons chopped cilantro

4 to 8 lime wedges

Transfer the roasted vegetables to the Dutch oven and set on the stovetop over medium-high heat. Add the garlic, chicken stock, and corn tortilla, and bring to a boil. Lower the heat and let simmer for 30 minutes. Remove from the heat and cover with the lid.

Using tongs, transfer the chicken thighs from the soup to a cutting board and let cool slightly. Separate the meat from the bones, discarding the bones. Shred the chicken into large chunks, then return the shredded meat to the soup.

To make the chipotle crema: Whisk together the sour cream, heavy cream, lime juice, chipotle powder, and salt until combined. Cover and set aside. Refrigerate until ready to use or up to 3 days if making ahead.

To serve, ladle the hot soup into bowls and drizzle with crema. Top with crispy tortilla strips, avocado slices, and cilantro. Garnish with lime wedges for squeezing into the soup.

Prep Time: 10 minutes, plus
15 minutes marinating time
Cook Time: 0 minutes

Butter Lettuce with Citrus Vinaigrette

There is no better lettuce than butter lettuce. Also known as butterhead, Boston, or Bibb lettuce, the leaves are smooth and mildly sweet, sturdy enough to carry a vinaigrette without wilting too much. A ripe avocado complements the buttery flavor, and a bit of citrus in the vinaigrette balances out the sweetness. This is a classic salad that's a perfect accompaniment to a spring or summer meal.

1 head butter lettuce

1½ tablespoons fresh lime juice

1 tablespoon Dijon mustard

1½ teaspoons champagne vinegar

1 teaspoon honey

Kosher salt and freshly ground black pepper

1 small garlic clove, sliced

½ small shallot, thinly sliced

½ cup extra-virgin olive oil

1 ripe avocado, cut into ½-inch cubes

Separate the lettuce leaves and rinse with cold water. Tear the larger leaves in half. Dry the lettuce leaves thoroughly using a salad spinner or with a clean kitchen towel.

To make the vinaigrette, whisk together the lime juice, mustard, vinegar, honey, ¼ teaspoon salt, and a pinch of pepper. Add the garlic and shallots and let sit for 15 to 20 minutes. Remove the garlic and shallots from the vinegar, discarding the garlic but reserving the shallots in a separate bowl. Slowly drizzle the olive oil into the vinegar mixture, whisking vigorously until completely combined. Store in an airtight container in the refrigerator until ready to use or up to 5 days. Whisk or shake vigorously to recombine before using. Serve at room temperature.

In a large bowl, drizzle the lettuce with the 2 to 3 tablespoons of the vinaigrette and toss well to coat the lettuce. Add the shallots and avocado and gently toss to combine. Season with additional salt and pepper. Serve immediately.

Kale Salad with Daikon Radish and Green Goddess Dressing

Daikon radishes and mangoes elevate the kale salad from ordinary to extraordinary. There is no ho-hum reaction when you combine this with the bright flavors of Green Goddess dressing. This salad is healthy, satisfying, and flavorful. A word to the wise—the daikon radishes can have a fairly pungent odor when pickled. Add a lemon slice or two to the brine and rinse them with some cold water before using.

Radish Brine

¼ cup rice vinegar

¼ cup water

1 teaspoon honey

1 teaspoon salt

½ cup peeled, cubed daikon radish

Dressing

¼ cup canola oil

3 tablespoons Greek yogurt

2 tablespoons fresh lemon juice

1 tablespoon champagne vinegar

1 teaspoon honey

½ teaspoon Dijon mustard

1 anchovy fillet

½ small shallot

¼ cup flat-leaf parsley

2 tablespoons basil

2 tablespoons chives

1 tablespoon tarragon

½ teaspoon kosher salt

Salad

1 ripe mango

2 cups baby kale leaves, rinsed and dried

½ grapefruit, sliced

To make the radish brine: Whisk together the rice vinegar, water, honey, and salt until combined.

Place the radish cubes into a large glass jar. Pour the brine over the radish cubes and place in the refrigerator overnight or up to 1 week.

Use a slotted spoon to remove the quick pickled radish cubes, rinse briefly with cold water, and set on a paper towel–lined plate to drain briefly.

To make the dressing: In a blender or food processor, add the canola oil, yogurt, lemon juice, champagne vinegar, honey, mustard, anchovy, shallot, parsley, basil, chives, tarragon, and salt and blend until smooth and emulsified, 1 to 2 minutes. This is best if used right away or within 2 days.

To make the salad: Cut the mango lengthwise on either side of the pit. Using a paring knife, score the flesh along the length and width, creating a lattice, being careful not to cut through the skin. Gently push on the skin to invert each mango half and push out the flesh, using a knife to cut into ¼-inch cubes.

In a large bowl, combine the kale and 2 tablespoons of the dressing and toss to coat. Add the radishes and mangoes and toss to coat. Transfer to a large platter or salad bowl and top with grapefruit slices. Use a spoon to drizzle 2 more tablespoons of dressing over the top.

Prep Time: 35 minutes, plus
30 minutes marinating time
and 15 minutes chilling time
Cook Time: 0 minutes

Marinated Vegetables

⅔ cup julienned carrots
(or thinly sliced)

½ cup thinly sliced English
cucumbers

¼ cup champagne vinegar

1 tablespoon honey

1 teaspoon flaky sea salt

Dressing

½ cup mayonnaise

1 tablespoon ketchup

1 tablespoon fresh
lemon juice

2 teaspoons sweet relish

1 teaspoon finely grated
shallot

½ teaspoon lemon zest

¼ teaspoon kosher salt

Pinch of freshly ground
black pepper

Dash of hot sauce

Dash of Worcestershire sauce

Salad

½ head iceberg lettuce,
washed, dried, and torn

1 Cherokee Purple or Black
Krim heirloom tomato,
quartered

½ cup black pitted olives,
halved

½ cup frozen peas, thawed
at room temperature

1 hard-boiled egg, peeled
and halved

8 ounces crabmeat
(preferably Dungeness,
or jumbo lump)

2 Meyer lemon wedges,
for garnish

Crab Louie Salad

Cole's dad loves Crab Louie, specifically at a no-frills restaurant in Santa Cruz called Gilda's Restaurant. I tried to honor the simplicity of the ingredients of that salad here, with just a few frills. I do recommend fussing over good heirloom tomatoes, such as Cherokee Purple or Black Krim, if you can find them. The finely cut, quick pickled carrots and cucumbers are a delicate and refreshing addition. In "lieu-ie" of Dungeness crabs, find a good quality jumbo-lump crabmeat, or bay shrimp.

To make the marinated vegetables: In a bowl, toss together the carrots, cucumbers, vinegar, honey, and salt. Cover and let marinate for at least 30 minutes at room temperature or up to 2 days in the refrigerator. When ready to use, drain off the liquid and discard before placing the vegetables on the salad.

To make the dressing: In a bowl, mix together the mayonnaise, ketchup, lemon juice, relish, shallot, lemon zest, salt, pepper, hot sauce, and Worcestershire until well combined. Cover and store in the refrigerator until ready to use or up to 4 days.

To make the salad: Place two serving dishes (rimmed plates or wide shallow bowls) in the refrigerator to chill for at least 15 minutes or in the freezer for 5 minutes.

Divide the lettuce between the serving dishes. Arrange the tomatoes, olives, peas, hard-boiled egg, carrots, and cucumbers on top of the lettuce. Top with a generous mound of crabmeat. Garnish with a lemon wedge and serve with the dressing on the side or drizzled over the top.

Little Gems with Watermelon Radish, Crispy Prosciutto, and Humboldt Fog

Little Gem lettuce leaves are cute and useful. They are on the small side so they can be left as whole leaves (or even halved lengthwise if desired). They have a delicate, sweet flavor, but with their sturdy stalks and wavy leaves they can store micro pockets of vinaigrette in every leaf and hold up to the weight of other ingredients. In this recipe the Little Gems are great for holding a little more of the sweet red wine vinaigrette as well as carrying a big wedge of creamy Humboldt Fog cheese on top. The crispy prosciutto brings home the flavor matrix with salt and crunch in a delicate, light package.

Vinaigrette

1½ tablespoons red wine vinegar

1½ teaspoons fresh lemon juice

1½ teaspoons granulated sugar

½ small garlic clove, mashed to a smooth paste

Pinch of kosher salt

Pinch of freshly ground black pepper

¼ cup extra-virgin olive oil

Salad

3 heads Little Gem lettuce, cored and leaves separated

2 ounces thinly sliced Prosciutto di Parma, cut in half crosswise

2 watermelon radishes, thinly sliced

2 ounces Humboldt Fog cheese (or goat cheese), cut into 2 wedges

Kosher salt and freshly ground black pepper

Lemon peels, for garnish (optional)

To make the vinaigrette: In a small bowl whisk together the red wine vinegar, lemon juice, sugar, garlic, salt, and pepper. Slowly drizzle in the olive oil, whisking vigorously until completely combined, and set aside.

To make the salad: Separate the lettuce leaves and rinse with cold water. Dry the lettuce leaves thoroughly but gently, using a salad spinner or a kitchen towel. Set aside.

In a large skillet over medium heat, add the prosciutto and cook until crispy and golden, 3 to 5 minutes. Transfer to a paper towel–lined plate to drain and set aside.

In a large bowl, add the lettuce and radishes, drizzle with the vinaigrette, and toss well to combine and coat. Divide the lettuce onto plates, topping with a wedge of the cheese and crispy prosciutto bits. Season with salt and pepper. Garnish with the lemon peels, if using. Serve immediately.

Cook's Note: If you are unable to find Little Gem lettuce, you can substitute hearts of romaine or heirloom romaine.

Prep Time: 10 minutes,
plus 15 minutes chilling time
Cook Time: 10 minutes

Classic Wedge Salad with Blue Cheese and Bacon

This is a simple but always refreshing and satisfying salad. The key is to keep the lettuce cold up until serving. Chilling the plates helps ensure a crisp, cool crunch—a step you could probably skip if you were hosting a large dinner party, but if it's just you two chickens, it's easy to go the extra mile.

Dressing

⅓ cup sour cream

⅓ cup mayonnaise

2 tablespoons crumbled blue cheese

1 tablespoon whole milk or heavy cream

1 teaspoon apple cider vinegar

1 teaspoon granulated sugar

½ teaspoon finely grated shallot

¼ teaspoon kosher salt

¼ teaspoon freshly ground black pepper

Salad

3 slices thick-cut bacon

1 head iceberg lettuce, quartered lengthwise and outer leaves removed

¼ cup cherry tomatoes, halved

2 tablespoons chopped chives

2 tablespoons crumbled blue cheese

Pinch of kosher salt

Pinch of freshly ground black pepper

To make the dressing: Whisk to combine all of the ingredients until well blended. Use right away or store in an airtight container in the refrigerator for up to 4 days. Whisk to recombine before using.

To make the salad: Place the serving dishes in the refrigerator to chill for at least 15 minutes or in the freezer for 5 minutes.

In a cast-iron skillet, place the bacon slices side by side. Place the skillet over medium-low heat and cook until the bacon has rendered its fat and the slices can be easily released from the pan with tongs. Flip the bacon slices over and cook until evenly browned and crispy on both sides, flipping and turning as needed. The whole process should take 8 to 10 minutes. Transfer to paper towels to drain and blot to remove excess fat. Cut the bacon into small pieces.

Place the lettuce wedges on the chilled plates and spoon the dressing over the top. Evenly distribute the bacon pieces, tomatoes, chive, and blue cheese crumbles over the wedges. Sprinkle with the salt and pepper.

Roasted Beet Salad with Baby Arugula, Feta, and Edamame

This salad appeals to all of the senses and is a favorite at any time of year. The natural sweetness of the colorful roasted beets complements the tangy feta cheese and peppery arugula. The sunflower seeds provide a delicate and salty crunch and the edamame bring a tiny and chewy bite packed with plant-based protein. You will enjoy this salad so much that you will forget how healthy it is.

Salad

2 golden beets, rinsed and scrubbed

2 red or Chioggia beets, rinsed and scrubbed

2 tablespoons olive oil

½ teaspoon kosher salt

⅓ cup frozen shelled edamame

2 cups baby arugula

¼ teaspoon freshly ground black pepper

2 ounces feta cheese, crumbled

¼ cup salted toasted sunflower seeds

Flaky sea salt

Vinaigrette

1½ tablespoons extra-virgin olive oil

2 teaspoons champagne vinegar

To make the salad: Preheat the oven to 425°F. Line a baking sheet with aluminum foil.

Trim off the beets' root ends and the leafy tops. Leave the beets whole.

Set the beets on the baking sheet and drizzle with olive oil. Sprinkle with ¼ teaspoon of the kosher salt, cover with another sheet of foil, and seal the edges. Roast for about 45 minutes, until the beets are tender. When cool enough to handle, remove the skins with a paring knife, then let cool completely. Cut into bite-size chunks or wedges.

While the beets are cooking, boil the edamame in salted boiling water for 5 minutes, then drain well. Let cool slightly.

To make the vinaigrette: In a small bowl, whisk together the olive oil and vinegar until well blended.

In a large mixing bowl, add the arugula. Season with the remaining ¼ teaspoon kosher salt and the freshly ground black pepper. Drizzle with the vinaigrette and toss to combine. Transfer to a serving platter or bowl. Top with the roasted beet wedges, edamame, and crumbled feta, and sprinkle with the sunflower seeds and sea salt.

Charred Radicchio, Avocado, and Pear Salad with Buttermilk Dressing

Radicchio is ideal for charring because it is firm enough to hold its shape and the charring mellows the natural bitterness. The avocado is smooth and silky, while the pear adds a sweet, juicy, and mild crunch. We love the buttermilk dressing, but a vinaigrette (on page 67 or 72) would also be a great alternative.

Buttermilk Dressing

⅓ cup buttermilk

¼ cup sour cream

2 tablespoons mayonnaise

1½ tablespoons chopped fresh chives

1 small garlic clove, minced

1 teaspoon apple cider vinegar

¼ teaspoon kosher salt

Pinch of freshly ground black pepper

Salad

1 small head radicchio

1½ tablespoons olive oil

1 Anjou pear

1 teaspoon fresh lemon juice

1 ripe avocado, cubed

¼ teaspoon kosher salt, plus more as needed

Pinch of freshly ground black pepper, plus more as needed

To make the buttermilk dressing: In a bowl, whisk together the buttermilk, sour cream, mayonnaise, chives, garlic, vinegar, salt, and pepper until well blended. Cover and refrigerate until ready to use or up to 3 days if making ahead. Serve chilled.

To make the salad: Wash and dry the radicchio. Remove any wilted outer leaves. Cut into wedges.

Heat a cast-iron or heavy skillet over high heat and add the oil. Place the radicchio cut side down in the skillet and cook until beginning to brown, about 4 minutes per side. Season with the salt and pepper and set aside.

When ready to serve the salad, core and quarter the pear. Cut the pear quarters into thin slices about ¼ inch thick. Drizzle with the lemon juice.

To assemble the salad, place the charred radicchio on a serving dish surrounded by the avocado cubes and pear slices. Drizzle with the chilled buttermilk dressing. Season with additional salt and pepper.

Prep Time: 2½ hours (includes
2 hours marinating time)
Cook Time: 40 minutes
(includes cooling time)

Grilled Curry Chicken Salad Lettuce Cups

Prepare the components of this salad on a Sunday so that you can jump-start a healthy week. A butter lettuce cup makes a yummy, neat little package for the grilled curry chicken that sits on top of the salad, but you could easily dice the grilled chicken and toss it in with all of the other ingredients. Eat it on top of a bed of greens if you prefer, or you could just eat it straight out of the storage container while standing next to the fridge, like we inevitably do every time.

Chicken

2 tablespoons canola oil

1 tablespoon honey

1 tablespoon fresh
lemon juice

2 teaspoons Dijon mustard

2 teaspoons curry powder

1 garlic clove, minced

1 teaspoon peeled, finely
grated fresh ginger

½ teaspoon kosher salt

¼ teaspoon freshly ground
pepper

2 small skinless boneless
chicken breasts

Aioli

⅓ cup mayonnaise

1 small garlic clove, minced

1 teaspoon curry powder

1 teaspoon fresh lemon juice

¼ teaspoon kosher salt,
plus more as needed

1 Granny Smith apple,
peeled and cubed

2 celery stalks, diced

½ cup purple grapes, halved

¼ cup chopped cashews

12 leaves butter lettuce,
gently washed and patted dry

To make the chicken: In a small saucepan over medium heat, add the oil, honey, lemon juice, mustard, curry powder, garlic, ginger, salt, and pepper and stir to combine. Cook for about 2 minutes or until just beginning to simmer. Remove from the heat and let cool to room temperature. Place the chicken breasts in a zippered bag or container with a lid. Pour the cooled marinade over the chicken and seal the bag or container before placing it in the refrigerator overnight or for at least 2 hours to marinate.

Preheat an outdoor grill or grill pan to medium heat. Remove the chicken breasts from the marinade and grill for about 5 minutes on each side until golden brown and the internal temperature reaches 165°F. Transfer the chicken to a plate and let rest for 5 minutes. Cover and place in the refrigerator to cool for at least 30 minutes (or up to 3 days if making ahead) before slicing in half crosswise, then cutting into thin lengthwise strips. Set aside.

To make the aioli: In a bowl, stir to combine the mayonnaise, garlic, curry powder, lemon juice, and salt. Add the apple, celery, grapes, and cashews and toss to combine. Season with additional salt to taste. If making ahead, store in an airtight container in the refrigerator for up to 3 days.

To serve, spoon the curry aioli mixture into the lettuce cups and top with a few slices of chicken.

Greek-Style Panzanella

Panzanella is a classic Italian bread and ripe summer tomato salad. When I thought of panzanella as a bruschetta in salad form, I was inspired to make the panzanella more like *dakos*, which is a Greek version of bruschetta. *Dakos* is comprised of a very crunchy toast called barley rusks that is topped with tomatoes, feta, olive oil, oregano, and often olives and capers as well. The oil and tomato juice seep into the rusks, making them softer and super tasty. If rusks aren't to be found in your local store, try a hearty multigrain rustic country bread.

Dressing

⅓ cup extra-virgin olive oil

1 tablespoon fresh
lemon juice

1 teaspoon lemon zest

1 teaspoon caper juice

1 teaspoon honey

¼ teaspoon kosher salt

Pinch of freshly ground
black pepper

Salad

12 ounces cherry tomatoes,
preferably heirloom, halved

1¼ teaspoons kosher salt

3 cups cubed rustic country
bread (or rusks)

1½ tablespoons olive oil

½ teaspoon dried oregano

½ small red onion, diced

½ English cucumber, peeled
and cubed

⅓ cup kalamata olives,
halved and pitted

2 ounces feta cheese,
crumbled

¼ cup chopped mint

2 tablespoons chopped basil

1 tablespoon chopped
flat-leaf parsley

To make the dressing: In a small container that can be sealed with a lid, add the olive oil, lemon juice, lemon zest, caper juice, honey, salt, and pepper. Shake until emulsified. Set aside.

To make the salad: Preheat the oven to 325°F.

In a large bowl, add the tomatoes and sprinkle with 1 teaspoon of the salt and toss to combine. Let sit for 15 to 20 minutes to extract juices that will be used to soften the bread.

On a rimmed baking sheet, spread out the bread cubes and drizzle with the olive oil, tossing to combine. Sprinkle with the remaining ¼ teaspoon of salt and the oregano and bake for 10 to 15 minutes, or until golden brown. Set aside to cool.

In a small bowl, add the onion and cover with cold water. Let sit for about 5 minutes, then drain, pat dry, and set aside.

Add the toasted bread to the bowl of tomatoes and gently toss together. Add the onion, cucumber, olives, feta, mint, basil, and parsley. Pour in the dressing and gently toss again until well combined. Let rest for 10 to 15 minutes to marinate before serving, tossing occasionally.

Prep Time: 20 minutes, plus
30 minutes marinating time
Cook Time: 25 minutes

Soba Noodle Salad with Tofu and Charred Green Onions

This soba noodle salad is a light and refreshing dish that can be served chilled or warm. If serving warm, you could add a poached or soft-boiled egg on top and call it supper. To enhance the chilled version with even more flavor and a little crunch, serve with some julienned or finely sliced cucumbers and carrots.

2 tablespoons soy sauce

1 tablespoon peeled, minced fresh ginger

2 teaspoons rice vinegar

2 teaspoons fresh lemon juice

1 teaspoon fish sauce

1 teaspoon white miso (optional)

1 small garlic clove, smashed

1 teaspoon honey

1 (14-ounce) package extra firm tofu, drained and patted dry

1 bunch green onions

1½ tablespoons grapeseed or avocado oil

8 ounces dried soba noodles

3 tablespoons vegetable stock (or reserved noodle cooking water)

1 tablespoon chopped cilantro, for garnish

1 teaspoon black sesame seeds, for garnish

In a small bowl, whisk to combine the soy sauce, ginger, rice vinegar, lemon juice, fish sauce, miso, garlic, and honey.

Cut the tofu into 1-inch cubes. Place the tofu pieces side by side in a small rimmed baking dish. Pour the marinade over the tofu. Cover and place in the refrigerator for about 30 minutes to marinate, flipping pieces over halfway through.

Preheat the broiler to high. Line a baking sheet with aluminum foil.

Place the green onions on the prepared baking sheet. Drizzle with 1½ teaspoons of the oil and toss to coat. Spread into a single layer and broil until charred, about 4 minutes. Transfer to a plate and set aside to cool slightly, then cut crosswise into 1-inch pieces (or leave whole, if desired).

Bring a large pot of salted water to a boil. Add the soba noodles, stir, and cook for 4 to 6 minutes, until tender but not overly soft. Drain the noodles, reserving a ladleful of the noodle cooking water, if using, and rinse the noodles with very cold water until cool. Set aside.

Remove the tofu from the marinade, reserving the liquid. Stir the vegetable stock (or 3 tablespoons of the reserved cooking water) into the tofu marinade. Set aside.

Preheat a large deep skillet or wok over medium-high heat until hot. Add the remaining oil, swirling to coat. When the oil starts to shimmer, add the tofu and stir-fry, flipping occasionally, until lightly browned on most sides, 5 to 7 minutes.

Add the noodles and marinade mixture to the skillet. Turn down the heat to medium and stir-fry for 1 to 2 minutes, until warm and well combined.

Divide the noodles and tofu into two bowls. Top with the green onions and garnish with cilantro and black sesame seeds.

Cucumber Sandwich with Harissa Yogurt

This is like a dainty tea sandwich turned on its head with a little kick of heat from harissa, a spicy and aromatic chili paste used in North African and Middle Eastern cuisine. If you can't find it, try another chili paste such as gochujang or Sriracha.

⅓ English cucumber, peeled

2 ounces goat cheese, at room temperature

2 tablespoons plain Greek yogurt

1 tablespoon basil

1 small garlic clove

¼ teaspoon lime zest

1 tablespoon harissa

1 tablespoon extra-virgin olive oil

4 slices multigrain bread

Flaky sea salt and freshly ground black pepper

⅔ cup sunflower sprouts or pea shoots

1 ripe avocado, cut into ⅓-inch-thick slices

Using a sharp knife, cut the cucumber lengthwise into ¼-inch thick slices and place them between paper towels. Let stand for about 15 minutes to drain excess moisture.

In a food processor, pulse together the goat cheese, Greek yogurt, basil, garlic, and lime zest. Transfer to a small bowl and drizzle in the harissa and oil, giving it just a quick swirl so that streaks remain.

Using a small spatula or knife, spread the goat cheese mixture on two of the bread slices. Layer with the cucumbers. Season with sea salt and pepper, then add layers of sprouts and avocado. Top with the remaining slices of bread. Use a serrated knife to cut the sandwiches in half.

MAKES 4 SERVINGS

Prep Time: 20 minutes, plus
at least 2 hours pressing time
Cook Time: 45 minutes

Cold-Pressed Roasted Eggplant Sandwich with Parsley Pistachio Pesto

Two sandwiches have left their imprints in my heart, metaphorically speaking. One, a crispy coated baked (or fried) eggplant sandwich with a pistachio pesto from Trail's End Cafe, a local Concord, Massachusetts, restaurant. The other sandwich was a roasted delicata squash sandwich from Tartine Manufactory in San Francisco that I still dream about. It had a to-die-for cheese called Crescenza that melted into their delectable country loaf.

This recipe borrows elements from both of those beloved sandwiches but sets itself apart with a unique method of cold pressing, also used in a muffuletta sandwich, where the sandwich is kept under a heavy object in the refrigerator overnight for flavor-melding magic. Roasting the eggplant versus frying allows you to be able to eat this sandwich cold and make it ahead of time.

Eggplant and Red Peppers

1 firm eggplant (¾ to 1 pound), cut into ½-inch-thick rounds

¼ teaspoon kosher salt

2 to 3 tablespoons avocado oil

2 red bell peppers, stemmed, seeded, and quartered

Pesto

⅓ cup shelled raw pistachios

2 garlic cloves

¾ cup flat-leaf parsley

2 tablespoons grated Parmesan cheese

1 tablespoon water

To make the eggplant and red peppers: Preheat the oven to 475°F. Line two baking sheets with parchment paper or nonstick foil.

Arrange the eggplant slices in a single layer on one of the baking sheets. On the second baking sheet, arrange the peppers skin side up in a single layer. Use a pastry brush to generously coat both sides of the eggplant slices and peppers with avocado oil and season with salt. Place the baking sheets in the oven and roast for 30 to 40 minutes, flipping halfway through, until tender and brown. Broil for a few minutes to crisp up, if necessary. Set the eggplant aside to cool. (If making ahead, drizzle with a little of olive oil and store in an airtight container in the refrigerator for 1 to 2 days.)

Using tongs, transfer the peppers to a bowl, cover the bowl tightly with plastic wrap, and set aside. When cool enough to handle, peel the skins off and discard. Set the peppers aside to cool completely. (If making ahead, drizzle with a little olive oil and store in an airtight container in the refrigerator for 1 to 2 weeks.)

To make the pesto: Add the pistachios and garlic to a food processor and pulse a few times until broken into smaller pieces. Add the parsley, Parmesan, water, lemon juice, vinegar, salt, and pepper and pulse until

CONTINUED

CONTINUED

Cold-Pressed Roasted Eggplant Sandwich with Parsley Pistachio Pesto

2 teaspoons fresh lemon juice

1½ teaspoons rice vinegar

¼ teaspoon kosher salt

¼ teaspoon freshly ground black pepper

3 tablespoons extra-virgin olive oil

Sandwich

1 pound ciabatta or rustic country bread loaf (about 5 by 12 inches), split in half lengthwise

2 to 3 tablespoons salted butter, at room temperature

4 to 5 ounces Crescenza or Stracchino cheese (or fresh mozzarella, sliced ¼ inch thick)

Cook's Note: Crescenza cheese, also known as Stracchino, is a type of Italian fresh cheese, typical of Lombardy, Piedmont, and Veneto. It is rich and creamy and mostly mellow with a hint of tanginess to it. It softens wonderfully at room temperature, making it perfect for this cold-pressed sandwich.

chopped. Use a spatula to scrape down the sides and bottom of the food processor bowl. Pour in the olive oil while pulsing just until the pesto comes together into a thick, finely textured paste. Set aside until ready to use or refrigerate, with plastic wrap pressed directly against the surface, in an airtight container for up to 5 days. Bring to room temperature and stir to recombine before using.

To make the sandwich: Spread the butter on the insides of the bread. Heat a large cast-iron skillet or griddle over medium-high heat. Place the bread in the pan, buttered side down, and cook for 3 to 5 minutes, or until lightly toasted.

To assemble the sandwich, spread the top half of the bread with the pesto. On the bottom half of the bread, spread a layer of the cheese, then add the roasted eggplant and red pepper slices. Close the sandwich with the top half of the bread, then wrap tightly in plastic wrap.

To cold-press the sandwich, place the wrapped sandwich under a flat, heavy object (for example, a baking dish filled with about 5 pounds of canned foods) for at least 2 hours at room temperature or up to 12 hours in the refrigerator.

To serve, remove the plastic wrap and use a sharp, serrated knife to cut the bread crosswise into four equal pieces.

Grilled Cheese with Gruyère and Caramelized Onions

A spread of whole grain mustard, mayonnaise, and horseradish on the outside of the bread forms a flavorful, tangy crust on the exterior of this grilled cheese. The duo of Gruyère and mozzarella optimizes both flavor and melty-ness. Adding caramelized onions isn't necessary, but I like the extra layer of texture, and they provide a nice balance to the slight aromatic kick of heat from the mustard and horseradish.

3 tablespoons salted butter

1 onion, sliced

¼ teaspoon granulated sugar

3 tablespoons whole grain mustard

1½ tablespoons mayonnaise

2 teaspoons prepared horseradish

4 slices fresh white bread (pain de mie or Pullman loaf)

3 ounces Gruyère, shredded

2 ounces mozzarella, shredded

In a skillet over medium-low heat, warm 1 tablespoon of the butter. Add the onion, sprinkle with sugar, and cook for 25 to 35 minutes, stirring occasionally, until golden brown and caramelized. Set aside.

In a small bowl, add the mustard, mayonnaise, and horseradish and stir to combine.

Place the bread slices on a cutting board and evenly distribute the mustard mixture over the top side of each slice of bread.

In a large skillet over medium heat, melt 1 tablespoon of the butter. Place 2 slices of the bread in the skillet, mustard side down. Working quickly, evenly distribute the cheeses and caramelized onion on top of the bread in the skillet. Top with the remaining slices of bread, mustard side up. Cook for 3 to 4 minutes, or until the bottom of the bread is golden brown.

Use a large spatula to carefully flip the sandwiches over while adding the remaining 1 tablespoon of butter to the skillet. Cook until the second side is golden brown and the cheese is melted, about 3 minutes.

Return the sandwiches to the cutting board and cut in half diagonally. Serve right away.

Open-Faced Niçoise-Style Tuna Melt

There's no sadder lunch than a tuna melt on soggy basic bread. That is not this sandwich. Good country bread with an assertive crunch (especially after getting toasted in the oven) not only holds up to the tuna salad mixture on top of it, but the tuna salad also melds with the complex flavors of the dough. Serving these as an open-faced tartine with fresh herbs, niçoise olives, and a little truffle oil makes this feel like a more elegant, grown-up lunch.

2 (5-ounce) cans tuna packed in olive oil, rinsed and drained

1 tablespoon Dijon mustard

1 teaspoon white truffle oil

½ teaspoon granulated sugar

½ teaspoon fresh lemon juice

¼ cup niçoise or kalamata olives, pitted and chopped

¼ cup cannellini beans, drained

1 tablespoon finely chopped flat-leaf parsley

1 tablespoon chopped green onion (about 1 stalk)

2 (¾-inch-thick) slices sourdough or rustic country bread

2 tablespoons salted butter, softened

Pinch of kosher salt

Pinch of freshly ground black pepper

2 vine tomatoes (Campari tomatoes), sliced ⅓ inch thick

2 ounces sharp provolone, thinly sliced

Preheat the oven to 450°F.

In a bowl, add the tuna, mustard, truffle oil, sugar, and lemon juice and stir with a fork, until the tuna is broken up into soft, small pieces and the mixture is well blended. Add the olives, beans, parsley, and green onion and mix until just incorporated. (If making ahead, transfer the tuna salad to an airtight container and store in the refrigerator for up to 2 days.)

Place the bread slices on a baking sheet. Spread the butter on top of the bread slices, season with the salt and pepper, and bake until lightly toasted, 3 to 5 minutes.

Preheat the broiler to low.

Divide the tuna salad evenly onto the toasted bread, spreading all the way to the edges of the bread. Use the back of a fork or spoon to gently press the tuna down to create a flat, even surface. Top with the tomato slices and cheese.

Return the baking sheet to the oven to broil for 5 to 10 minutes, until the cheese has melted and starts to brown, watching carefully so that it doesn't burn. Serve warm.

OPEN-FACED NIÇOISE

BLTTJ

GRILLED CHEESE

SAUSAGE AND PEPPER

MAKES 2 SERVINGS

Prep Time: 20 minutes
Cook Time: 1 hour, plus
30 minutes cooling time

Bacon, Lettuce, and Tomato with Tomato Jam *(BLTTJ)*

Ahh, a BLT. It's so simple and undeniably satisfying. This recipe is more like an instruction manual to build an advanced BLT sandwich. At the heart, it is still the same classic sandwich. Try it with fresh white bread from a local bakery that you can slice yourself—it's such a treat if you can find it. Butter lettuce is silky and flavorful, and the crispy thick-cut bacon adds a hearty crunch. The biggest upgrade is the beautiful, ripe heirloom tomatoes. The only addition—spicy tomato jam—plays well with mayo and adds a subtle layer of sweet tang and heat.

Tomato Jam

1 garlic clove, minced

2 tablespoons Sriracha

2 tablespoons granulated sugar

1 tablespoon honey

1 tablespoon olive oil

1 tablespoon soy sauce

¼ teaspoon kosher salt

¼ teaspoon fresh lime juice

1 pound plum tomatoes, halved lengthwise and cored

Sandwich

4 slices fresh white bread (such as pain de mie or Pullman loaf), cut ½ inch thick and lightly toasted

2 tablespoons mayonnaise

4 slices thick-cut bacon, cooked until crispy

4 leaves butter lettuce

4 thick slices heirloom tomato

To make the tomato jam: Preheat the oven to 375°F. Line a baking sheet with nonstick (or heavy-duty) aluminum foil.

In a small bowl, add the garlic, Sriracha, sugar, honey, olive oil, soy sauce, salt, and lime juice and stir to combine. Place the tomatoes on the baking sheet, cut side up. Drizzle with the Sriracha mixture. Bake for about 40 minutes, or until just starting to caramelize. When cool enough to handle, peel and discard the tomato skins. Transfer the tomatoes with all of the pan juices to a saucepan and use a potato masher or wooden spoon to break them up into a chunky paste. Simmer over low heat, stirring occasionally, until reduced to a jamlike consistency, about 20 minutes. Let cool before using. (If making ahead, store in an airtight container in the refrigerator for up to 1 week.)

To make the sandwich: Place two of the slices of bread down on a cutting board and spread the mayonnaise on the tops of both slices, distributing it evenly. Top both slices with equal amounts of the tomato, bacon, and lettuce. Spread 2 tablespoons of the spicy tomato jam onto the remaining two slices of bread, distributing it evenly. Close the sandwiches by placing each slice of bread, jam side down, on top of the lettuce. Use a serrated knife to cut the sandwiches in half. Serve right away.

Cook's Note: Use the leftover spicy tomato jam as a fun alternative to ketchup. It would also make an excellent secondary dip option for the Crispy Duck Fat Potatoes with Horseradish Crème Fraîche (page 134) or as a milder substitute for the harissa in the Cucumber Sandwich with Harissa Yogurt (page 87).

Sweet Italian Sausage and Pepper Sandwich

This sandwich transports me to carefree evenings in late summer when several neighborhood families would caravan to a nearby Italian festival, complete with rides, games, prizes, and so many delicious Italian homemade dishes. The wafting aroma of the sausage grilling, bread toasting, and onions and peppers sautéing would draw us into a stand where an extended family worked to assemble and proudly serve this rustic sandwich. It is now our family tradition to make it at home all year-round, with a few minor additions.

2 tablespoons olive oil

1 large sweet yellow onion, julienned

1 red bell pepper, julienned

2 large sweet Italian sausages

2 tablespoons salted butter, softened

2 tablespoons Dijon mustard

1 teaspoon honey

2 large crusty Italian sandwich rolls or 1 (8-ounce) French baguette, cut in half lengthwise

⅓ cup baby arugula

2 teaspoons red wine vinegar

4 ounces fresh mozzarella, sliced

In a large sauté pan over medium heat, warm the oil. Add the onion and cook for 15 to 20 minutes, stirring often, until softened and translucent. Add the pepper and continue to cook while stirring until the onions start to caramelize, about 15 minutes. If the onion looks dry, stir in some water while cooking, 1 tablespoon at a time. Set aside.

On a grill pan over medium-high heat, cook the sausages for 5 to 10 minutes on each side, until just starting to brown.

Using tongs, transfer the sausages to a cutting board. When cool enough to handle, butterfly the sausages by cutting lengthwise to split them open, without slicing all the way through. Return the butterflied sausages to the grill pan, cut sides down, and cook until lightly browned, about 5 minutes.

Preheat the broiler.

In a small bowl, mix together the butter, mustard, and honey. Spread the mixture over the cut sides of each roll. Place the rolls, cut side up, on a baking sheet and broil until lightly toasted, about 2 minutes.

In a small bowl, add the arugula and vinegar and toss to combine. Set aside.

Transfer the bottom halves of the rolls to serving plates. Place the sliced mozzarella on the top halves of the rolls. Return the baking sheet to the oven to broil for an additional 3 to 5 minutes, or until the cheese is melted.

Meanwhile, divide the sausages and onion among the bottom halves of the rolls. Top with the dressed arugula. Close the sandwiches with the top halves of the rolls, cheese side down. Serve warm.

French Dip Sandwich with Au Jus

This old-school classic is upgraded with caramelized onions, creamy horseradish spread, melted Gruyère, and an au jus dipping sauce that keeps you coming back for more. Juicy deli roast beef and the best French baguette you can find will make this a new (old-time) favorite. The dipping sauce and caramelized onions can be prepared ahead of time so that you can heat, assemble, and enjoy this for lunch or dinner.

Au Jus

1 tablespoon salted butter

1 large onion, preferably Vidalia, thinly sliced

Pinch of kosher salt

¼ teaspoon freshly ground black pepper

1 garlic clove, minced

2 tablespoons red wine

1½ cups beef stock

1 tablespoon Worcestershire sauce

Horseradish Spread

3 tablespoons sour cream

1½ tablespoons mayonnaise

2 teaspoons prepared horseradish

Sandwich

1 (8-ounce) French baguette

¾ to 1 pound thinly sliced medium rare deli roast beef

1 tablespoon salted butter, melted

1 cup shredded Gruyère (4 ounces)

To make the au jus: In a large sauté pan over medium-low heat, melt the butter. Add the onion and salt and cook, stirring occasionally, until softened and lightly browned, about 20 minutes. Season with pepper. Remove about two-thirds of the cooked onion and set aside. Add the garlic to the pan with the remaining onion and cook until fragrant, about 1 minute. Add the wine and cook, while stirring, until mostly evaporated. Add the beef stock and Worcestershire and let simmer over low heat for about 25 minutes. Set a sieve over a bowl and strain the au jus, pressing down on the onion to release any additional liquid. Discard the strained solids. Keep the au jus warm in a bowl wide enough for dipping to serve with the sandwiches. (If making ahead, let cool, store in airtight containers, and refrigerate for up to 2 days.)

To make the horseradish spread: Combine the sour cream, mayonnaise, and horseradish in a small bowl.

To make the sandwich: Preheat the oven to 375°F. Line a baking sheet with aluminum foil.

Cut the baguette in half crosswise, then cut both pieces in half through the middle.

Brush the insides of the baguette tops and bottoms with the melted butter and place them, cut sides up, on the baking sheet. Bake until lightly toasted, about 4 minutes. Transfer the bottom halves of the baguette to a plate and set aside.

On the top halves, add the cheese. Return the baking sheet to the oven and bake until the cheese is just melted, 3 to 4 minutes.

While the cheese is melting, spread the horseradish mixture onto the bottom halves of the baguette.

Working one slice at a time, dip the roast beef slices into the warm au jus before transferring them onto the sandwich bottoms, bunching up or fanning each slice as you place it onto the bread. Top with the reserved onion and finish with the top half of the baguette.

Serve the sandwiches warm with the au jus on the side.

Starters & Sides

Radishes with Thyme Butter

The simplicity of a fresh radish is truly appreciated here. If you serve the radishes without a baguette, you can even leave the tops of the radishes on for easier handling, serving them halved with the herb-infused butter.

3 tablespoons salted butter, softened

1 tablespoon chopped thyme

Baguette slices, warmed

½ bunch radishes, tops removed and thinly sliced

Coarse sea salt, for serving

In a small bowl, mix together the butter and thyme. Transfer to a dip bowl, smoothing the top with the flat side of a knife. Cover and store in the refrigerator until ready to use.

To serve, spread the thyme butter on warm baguette slices, top with sliced radishes, and sprinkle with coarse sea salt.

Prep Time: 15 minutes,
plus overnight chilling time
Cook Time: 50 minutes.
plus cooling time

Caponata

Caponata is a Sicilian dish that can be served as a salad, side dish, or antipasto relish. Plate it with crostini toasts and burrata drizzled with olive oil as an assemble-it-yourself appetizer. If entertaining, you could make a nice spread with caponata, Sweet and Sour Cipollini Onions (page 121), and an antipasto platter. Try using it as a sauce base to bake an egg, in the style of Tomato Curry Baked Eggs (page 39).

¼ cup olive oil, plus more if needed

2 small, firm eggplants, cut into ½-inch cubes

1 garlic clove, minced

1 small onion, diced

½ cup thinly sliced celery

1 teaspoon chopped thyme

2 anchovy fillets, chopped

¾ cup canned crushed tomatoes

3 tablespoons red wine vinegar

1 teaspoon kosher salt

½ teaspoon granulated sugar

½ teaspoon freshly ground black pepper

⅔ cup pitted black olives, chopped

⅓ cup pitted green olives, halved

¼ cup diced roasted red peppers

2 tablespoons toasted pine nuts

1 tablespoon capers with juice, chopped

1 teaspoon coarsely chopped basil

1 teaspoon coarsely chopped flat-leaf parsley

Heat 2 tablespoons of the olive oil in a large heavy sauté pan over medium-high heat until hot. Add the eggplant and sauté, while stirring, until browned on all sides and cooked through, about 10 minutes. Add more olive oil as the cooking progresses if the pan looks dry. Transfer to a bowl and set aside.

In the same pan, heat the remaining 2 tablespoons of olive oil over medium heat until hot. Add the garlic, onion, and celery and cook until the onion is softened and starting to brown, about 5 minutes. Add the thyme and anchovies and cook and stir until the anchovies start to melt, about 2 minutes.

Add the tomatoes, vinegar, salt, sugar, and pepper, and bring to a boil. Turn down the heat to low and let simmer, stirring occasionally, until thickened, 20 to 30 minutes. Remove from the heat and stir in the eggplant, olives, red peppers, pine nuts, capers, basil, and parsley. Let cool completely before storing in an airtight container in the refrigerator overnight or up to 2 days in advance.

Serve at room temperature.

Cook's Note: Caponata is ideal to make ahead, as the flavors improve from marinating at least overnight.

MAKES 6 ROLLS,
ENOUGH FOR 4 SERVINGS

Prep Time: 35 minutes
Cook Time: 0 minutes

Fresh Thai Spring Rolls with Peanut Dipping Sauce

Fresh spring rolls add a fresh, light element that is colorful and delicious as an appetizer, snack, lunch, or dinner. The peanut sauce and vegetable filling can be made ahead of serving and stored in airtight containers until ready to assemble. These are a great option when a vegetarian or vegan item is desired, but they are loved by all.

Dipping Sauce

¼ cup peanut butter

¼ cup coconut milk

2 tablespoons soy sauce

1 teaspoon fresh lime juice

1 small garlic clove, minced

2 dashes hot sauce

2 tablespoons water, plus more if needed

Spring Rolls

6 (8½-inch) rice paper wrappers

1 small bunch Thai basil leaves

1 small bunch mint leaves

6 leaves butter lettuce

1 cup shredded red cabbage

2 carrots, julienned

1 cup pea shoots or bean sprouts

To make the dipping sauce: Whisk together the peanut butter, coconut milk, soy sauce, lime juice, garlic, hot sauce, and water until smooth and well blended. (If making ahead, store in an airtight container and refrigerate for up to 5 days. Serve at room temperature.)

To make the spring rolls: Set the rice paper wrappers alongside a large shallow bowl filled with lukewarm water. Prepare and arrange the remaining ingredients in separate dishes in an assembly-line fashion.

Working one at a time, dip a rice paper wrapper in the water for about 5 seconds, then lift, letting the excess water drip back into the bowl. Place the wrapper on a clean, dry work surface and begin filling by placing a few Thai basil leaves and mint leaves in the center of the rice paper wrapper. Continue by topping it with a lettuce leaf, cabbage, carrots, and pea shoots.

Gently holding the filling ingredients in place, fold the bottom of the rice paper wrapper over the ingredients and press down to create a seal. Fold in both sides of the wrapper toward the center so the ends of the filling are tucked in and continue to gently roll as tightly as possible. Place the assembled roll, seam side down on a serving dish. Continue to assemble each roll in the same manner, making sure to leave space between each assembled roll, so they do not stick together.

To serve, use a sharp knife to cut them in half. Serve with the dipping sauce on the side. To make ahead, individually wrap whole rolls tightly in plastic wrap and store in the refrigerator for up to 1 day.

Cook's Note: Soaking the rice paper wrappers in warm water turns them into soft, pliable, and sticky vehicles for fresh vegetables dipped in peanut sauce. Once soaked, however, the wrappers are fragile, so you will need to work swiftly. Making an assembly line will help set you up for success. A few practice rolls will give you the feel for it. Much like when making a burrito, overfilling is for advanced users only, so start small and work your way up from there!

Prep Time: 25 minutes,
plus 1 hour marinating time
Cook Time: 1 hour, 15 minutes

Dad's Grilled Vegetable Medley

No summertime family gathering would be complete without a bountiful tray of my Dad's signature grilled vegetables. The marinade brings out the best in all of the vegetables, and the grilling adds the char and caramelization that makes it so appealing to even nonvegetable lovers.

Marinade

½ cup soy sauce

½ cup balsamic vinegar

¼ cup canola oil

1 tablespoon Worcestershire sauce

1 teaspoon hot sauce

Juice of ½ lemon

1 teaspoon onion powder

½ teaspoon freshly ground black pepper

Vegetables

3 large portobello mushrooms

2 eggplants, cut crosswise into ½-inch-thick rounds

3 zucchini, cut ½ inch thick on the diagonal

2 yellow squash, cut ½ inch thick on the diagonal

1 large sweet potato, peeled and cut ½ inch thick on the diagonal

2 very large carrots, peeled and cut ½ inch thick on the diagonal

1 red onion, cut crosswise into ½-inch-thick rings

3 tablespoons canola oil

To make the marinade: Whisk to combine the soy sauce, balsamic vinegar, canola oil, Worcestershire, hot sauce, lemon juice, onion powder, and pepper. Set aside.

To make the vegetables: Wipe the mushrooms clean with a damp cloth or paper towel and cut them into slices ½ inch thick.

Place the eggplant, zucchini, and yellow squash in a large roasting pan. In a separate pan, add the sweet potatoes, carrots, onion, and mushrooms.

Pour the marinade into the pans to cover and coat the vegetables. Cover both pans with plastic wrap and set aside for 1 hour at room temperature.

Preheat an outdoor grill to medium-high heat. Prepare an aluminum foil tray about 12 by 16 inches by folding up the edges of a piece of nonstick (or heavy-duty) aluminum foil. Place the foil tray directly on the grill.

Working in batches, place the sweet potatoes, carrots, and onion on the foil tray. Using a spatula or tongs, push the vegetables around every few minutes to avoid sticking. Grill until caramelized and golden brown, 10 to 15 minutes, then flip the vegetables over and continue grilling until golden brown on the other side. Discard the foil and transfer the vegetables to a serving platter.

Prepare another foil tray about 12 by 12 inches and set it on the grill. Place the mushrooms on the foil tray and grill until they release their juices and start to firm up, about 2 minutes. Carefully flip the mushrooms over and cook for another 2 minutes on the other side. Transfer to the serving platter.

Using a silicone brush, coat both sides of the vegetables with the canola oil. Grill the eggplant, zucchini, and yellow squash slices until char lines are visible, about 3 minute on each side. Flip the vegetables over, brush with some of the marinade from the pan, and repeat. Transfer to the serving platter.

Serve warm or at room temperature. If making ahead, drizzle lightly with olive oil and store in an airtight container in the refrigerator for up to 3 days.

Cook's Note: Grilling on an outdoor grill is ideal, however, an indoor grill pan can also be used. Cook vegetables on an indoor grill pan over medium-high heat, flipping occasionally, until golden brown and caramelized.

Fromage Fort Crostini

Fromage fort, which means "strong cheese," is a great way to clean out the cheese drawer and a good excuse to open a bottle of champagne. This fromage fort welcomes and benefits from a variety of cheeses with varying flavors and textures. The black garlic adds a sweet umami flavor, and the fresh tarragon blends in a mellow note of licorice.

Crostini

1½ tablespoons salted butter, melted

1½ tablespoons extra-virgin olive oil

12 slices baguette, ¾ inch thick and lightly toasted

¼ teaspoon kosher salt

Pinch of freshly ground black pepper

Cheese

6 ounces assorted leftover cheese (preferably a mixture of hard and soft, discarding rinds)

2 or 3 black garlic cloves

¼ cup dry white wine or sparkling white wine, preferably brut champagne

1½ teaspoons kirsch or brandy

1 teaspoon roughly chopped tarragon leaves

Pinch of kosher salt

Pinch of freshly ground black pepper

To make the crostini, preheat the oven to 400°F. Combine the butter and olive oil and use a pastry brush to lightly coat both sides of the bread and arrange on a baking sheet. Season with the salt and pepper. Bake for about 6 minutes, flipping with a spatula halfway through, until lightly toasted on both sides. Set aside until ready to use. (To make ahead, let cool completely before storing in an airtight container at room temperature for up to 1 day.)

To make the cheese: Preheat the broiler.

In a food processor, process the cheese, garlic, wine, kirsch, tarragon, salt, and pepper until cohesive and creamy, about 1 minute. Spread the cheese mixture onto the crostini and transfer them to a baking sheet. Place under the broiler for 2 to 3 minutes, until the cheese is golden brown and bubbly. Serve warm.

Dinner Rolls

I love good bread, from a rustic, artisan loaf to the humble, soft dinner roll. I hope this dinner roll recipe will be an approachable way for you to jump into baking fresh bread, and you'll see it is so much more than just a filling side at dinner. These rolls are great for hosting or for taking to an event as a guest. The overnight rise gives these rolls a superior cloudlike texture. The flavor is rich but not too greasy or too sweet—they taste fresh and wholesome.

1 cup whole milk

1 package active dry yeast (2¼ teaspoons)

1 teaspoon plus 2 tablespoons granulated sugar

2 eggs

3 cups all-purpose flour (360 grams), plus more for dusting

¾ teaspoon kosher salt

4 tablespoons unsalted butter, at room temperature

1 tablespoon vegetable oil, for greasing bowl

Canola oil spray, for coating the baking pan

1 teaspoon heavy cream

Flaky sea salt (optional)

2 teaspoons melted unsalted butter, for brushing on rolls after baking

Scald the milk by heating it to about 180°F. Let cool to 110°F.

Combine the warm milk with the yeast and 1 teaspoon of the sugar. Whisk and let it sit until a thick layer of foam has formed and the mixture has increased in volume, 10 to 15 minutes.

Add 1 egg to the yeast mixture and whisk to combine.

In a stand mixer fitted with the dough hook attachment, add the flour and gradually pour in the yeast mixture while mixing on low until just combined, about 2 minutes. Add the remaining sugar and the kosher salt and mix until combined and the dough starts to come together in a shaggy mass. Cover and let rest for 15 minutes.

Mix the rested dough on low speed, gradually adding the butter until fully incorporated; this can take up to 10 minutes. Continue to mix the dough until smooth, elastic, and somewhat springy, about 5 minutes more.

Lightly coat a clean bowl with oil, transfer the dough to the bowl, and cover with plastic wrap. Let rise at room temperature until almost doubled in volume, 1 to 1½ hours.

Spray a 9 by 13-inch baking pan lightly with the canola oil.

Turn the dough out onto a clean, very lightly floured work surface. Pat the dough into a rectangle, pressing out any air bubbles. Use a sharp knife or bench scraper to divide the dough into 12 equal pieces (about 2 ounces each). Work with one piece at a time, keeping the other pieces covered with plastic wrap or a clean towel. To shape each roll, grab one corner of the dough at a time, pulling it up and over the center of the dough, and repeat until the dough is gathered into a little round purse with a smooth bottom.

Cook's Note: If desired, you can divide your dough into fewer than 12 pieces to make bigger rolls. This amount of dough would make 9 good-size rolls for sandwiches or burgers.

Pinch the gathered dough on the top to create a seam. Flip the dough ball over so the seam side is down. Cup your hand over the dough and lightly drag the dough along your work surface toward you, keeping the smooth side face up and taut, letting friction seal the bottom seam. Repeat with the remaining dough pieces and place the rolls evenly spaced and seam side down into the prepared baking pan. Cover with plastic wrap and aluminum foil and refrigerate overnight, 8 to 12 hours.

Remove the rolls from the refrigerator and let sit at room temperature, still covered, until nearly doubled in size, about 45 minutes.

Meanwhile, preheat the oven to 375°F.

When proofed and ready to bake, the dough should look puffy and pillowlike. When pressed gently with a finger, the dough should spring back slightly but hold a slight indentation.

To prepare the egg wash, whisk the remaining egg with the heavy cream. Brush the tops of the rolls with the egg wash, then sprinkle with a pinch of sea salt. Bake for 15 minutes, or until golden brown on top. After baking, brush with the melted butter and serve warm.

Store leftover rolls, completely cooled, in an airtight container in the freezer for up to a month. To reheat the rolls, wrap in foil and place in a 325°F oven for 10 to 15 minutes, until warmed through.

Sausage Bread

MAKES ONE 13-INCH
SAUSAGE BREAD,
ENOUGH FOR 6 SERVINGS

Prep Time: 25 minutes,
plus 1 hour inactive time
Cook Time: 35 minutes

Our family is mildly obsessed (okay, completely obsessed) with this sausage bread. The house smells amazing when it is baking, and somehow everyone detaches themselves from their various devices and is drawn into the kitchen to steal a slice (or two, or three). When baking, some of the cheese will occasionally melt out onto the baking sheet and caramelize as it bakes. Those slices are the first to go. The ingredients are not extraordinary, but the finished product is an instant crowd favorite.

Homemade Pizza Dough
(page 42) or 1 pound
store-bought pizza dough

1 tablespoon olive oil

1 onion, preferably Vidalia,
chopped

10 ounces Italian sausage
(bulk or links, sausage
removed from casings)

1¼ cups shredded
mozzarella cheese

¼ cup of grated
Parmesan cheese

½ cup chopped flat-leaf
parsley

¼ teaspoon dried oregano

¼ teaspoon salt

¼ teaspoon freshly ground
black pepper

1 egg whisked with
1 tablespoon water,
for egg wash

1 tablespoon sesame seeds,
for garnish

Preheat the oven to 350°F. Line a baking sheet with parchment paper.

Place the pizza dough on a lightly floured surface and allow it to come to room temperature, about 2 hours, if it has been refrigerated.

Line a plate with paper towels. In a sauté pan over medium heat, add the olive oil and sauté the onion until translucent, 5 to 10 minutes. Transfer the onion to a bowl and set aside.

In the same pan over medium heat, cook the sausage, breaking it up with a spoon and stirring until brown. Transfer to the paper towel–lined plate.

On a lightly floured board, gently pat down the dough, and roll it into a rectangle about 13 by 18 inches. Arrange half of the cooked sausage in a row along the short edge of the dough. Top the row with half of the onion, half of the cheeses, and half of the parsley. Sprinkle with the oregano, salt, and pepper. Roll the dough until just the row of ingredients is covered and tucked in, then repeat with another row of the remaining sausage, onion, cheeses, and parsley. Continue to roll the dough to the end, positioning the seam on the bottom. Tuck the ends of the dough under the roll.

Carefully transfer the roll to the prepared baking sheet. Brush on the egg wash with a pastry brush, then sprinkle evenly with the sesame seeds. With a sharp knife, score the top of the dough with diagonal slits approximately 1 inch apart.

Bake for 30 to 35 minutes until the top is golden brown and the cheese begins to bubble. Allow to cool slightly, cut crosswise into 1-inch slices, and serve warm.

To make ahead, let the baked bread cool completely. Wrap the unsliced loaf in plastic wrap, then aluminum foil, and store in the refrigerator for up to 1 day or in the freezer for up to 1 month. If frozen, let thaw overnight in the refrigerator. Reheat on a baking sheet, loosely covered in foil, in a 350°F oven until hot, about 20 minutes.

Creamed Swiss Chard

When you think of old-world steakhouse fare, rich, velvety creamed spinach is sure to be a side dish on the table. Swiss chard is a very different plant than spinach, though, and is actually an offshoot of the beet family. It has similar nutritional value to spinach (so there's that!) but also has a slightly milder flavor and a little more bite in the stems, which will comfort traditional taste buds and sensibilities but will feel a little more adventurous. Serve with Creamy Mashed Potatoes (page 171) and Indoor Filet Mignon (page 179) to enjoy a fancy steakhouse dinner at home.

8 ounces Swiss chard
(½ bunch)

1 tablespoon olive oil

4 tablespoons salted butter

1 small shallot, minced

2 garlic cloves, minced

3 tablespoons
all-purpose flour

½ cup whole milk
(or half-and-half), at
room temperature,
plus more if needed

¼ cup grated
Parmesan cheese

¼ teaspoon kosher salt

¼ teaspoon freshly
ground black pepper

Pinch of nutmeg

Cook's Note: Additional milk may be needed to adjust the consistency, or half-and-half can be used.

Fold each Swiss chard leaf in half lengthwise and use a sharp knife to separate the tough stems and ribs from the leaves. Cut the stems and ribs into thin slices and set aside in a bowl. Coarsely chop the leaves into bite-size pieces and set aside in a separate bowl.

In a large skillet over medium heat, add the olive oil and 1 tablespoon of the butter. When the butter has melted, add the shallot and cook, stirring occasionally, until softened, about 3 minutes. Add the garlic and Swiss chard stems and turn the heat down to low. Cook, stirring often, until softened and just tender, about 5 minutes. Add the Swiss chard leaves, working in batches if necessary, and cook, tossing often, until all of the leaves are gently wilted, about 3 minutes.

Transfer the cooked chard to a large strainer or colander and press down to remove any excess liquid. Set aside.

In a large saucepan over medium heat, melt the remaining 3 tablespoons of butter. Add the flour and stir continuously until the mixture starts to foam. Gradually whisk in the milk and cook, stirring often, until smooth and thickened and no flour taste is evident, 10 to 15 minutes.

Add the Parmesan cheese, salt, pepper, nutmeg, and the cooked Swiss chard, stirring to combine, and cook until heated through. Serve warm.

If making ahead, store in an airtight container in the refrigerator for up to 1 day. To reheat, warm in a saucepan over low heat.

Shaved Fennel and Asparagus Salad with Orange and Warm Citrus Dressing

This refreshing salad is the perfect choice in spring and summer. It makes a wonderful, light lunch as well as a great accompaniment to delicate seafood and chicken dishes. Fennel and orange are meant to be together and the asparagus ribbons add a silky texture to this delicious and visually pleasing dish.

Salad

1 large fennel bulb, preferably with stalks and fronds attached

6 thick asparagus spears

1 navel orange

1 sprig of mint, for garnish

Dressing

½ teaspoon orange zest, plus additional for garnish

1½ tablespoons apple cider vinegar

1 teaspoon honey

3 tablespoons olive oil

¼ teaspoon kosher salt

Pinch of freshly ground black pepper

To make the salad: Prepare the fennel bulb by trimming the root end and stalks. Reserve some of the feathery fronds (if they appear fresh) for garnish. Reserve the remaining stalks for another use, such as chicken soup. Cut the bulb into quarters lengthwise, discarding any wilted outer layers. Using a mandoline or very sharp knife, cut each quarter of fennel crosswise into thin slices. Cover and set aside.

Prepare the raw asparagus by trimming off and discarding the woody ends. Lay the spear flat on a cutting board, hold it at the tips, and using a y-peeler, slice along the length of the asparagus spear to make ribbon-like shavings. Turn over the asparagus so that it lies flat and repeat on the other side, leaving the centermost slice with the asparagus tip still attached. Repeat with the remaining stalks.

To supreme the orange, slice off the top and bottom, then cut off the rind and pith, cutting along the curve of the orange from top to bottom. Continue trimming around the orange until all of the ribs and pith are removed. To make segments, cut inside the membrane, tilting the knife so that each section is sliced toward the center in a V to remove the segments. Set aside. Reserve the remainder of the orange after the segments are removed and squeeze 1½ tablespoons of juice to use for the citrus dressing.

To make the dressing: In a small saucepan over low heat, whisk to combine the orange zest and juice, vinegar, honey, oil, salt, and pepper, and heat until warm, about 3 minutes.

In a large mixing bowl, add the shaved fennel and asparagus ribbons. Add the warm citrus dressing and toss lightly. Transfer to a serving platter or bowl and top with the orange segments. Garnish with fennel fronds and a sprig of mint. Serve right away.

ROASTED CARROTS

CARAMELIZED LEEKS

CIPOLLINI ONIONS

GREEN BEANS AMANDINE

Roasted Carrots with Hot Honey

Hot honey doesn't mean warm honey, but spicy honey. You can buy hot honey, which is honey infused with chiles, as a condiment at some specialty stores or online. I highly recommend buying it, as I've found it to be a fun addition to so many foods—cheese, in particular—and even cocktails. For this recipe, however, I've made my own shortcut hot honey by quickly infusing the honey with red pepper flakes. It punches up these roasted carrots with a fantastic duo—a little sweet and a little heat!

2 tablespoons honey

2 teaspoons salted butter

2 teaspoons red pepper flakes, plus more for garnish (optional)

1 pound carrots with tops, scrubbed and tops removed, leaving 1 inch of greenery

1 tablespoon olive oil

Kosher salt, for garnish

Preheat the oven to 400°F. Line a baking sheet with parchment paper.

In a small saucepan over medium heat, add the honey, butter, and red pepper flakes and stir to combine. Turn the heat down to low and let simmer for about 10 minutes to infuse, stirring occasionally. Remove the pan from the heat and pour the honey through a strainer, discarding the red pepper flakes. Set aside.

Cut the carrots in half lengthwise.

Arrange the carrots in a single layer on the prepared baking sheet and drizzle with the olive oil. Roast the carrots for 30 to 40 minutes, turning with a spatula halfway through, until lightly browned and tender.

Transfer to a serving platter. Drizzle with the warm honey. Sprinkle with the sea salt and additional red pepper flakes, if desired.

Caramelized Leeks

Leeks are often overlooked as a side dish, but they shouldn't be. Try preparing them using this simple method, with a little enhancement from butter and lemon, to see the natural flavor of leeks in a whole new light. They are delicate and sweet, and they pair especially well with seafood and poultry entrées.

6 leeks, both white and green parts

2 teaspoons granulated sugar

½ teaspoon kosher salt

¼ teaspoon freshly ground black pepper

2 tablespoons salted butter

1 tablespoon olive oil

Juice and zest of 1 lemon

¼ cup chicken stock

Preheat the oven to 400°F. Line a rimmed baking sheet with aluminum foil.

Trim the leeks and cut them in half lengthwise. Rinse the leeks under running water, separating the layers slightly to help remove any dirt.

In a small bowl, mix together the sugar, salt, and pepper. Set aside.

Add the butter to the baking sheet and place in the oven to melt, about 2 minutes. While the butter is melting, sprinkle the sugar mixture over both sides of the leeks.

Remove the baking sheet from the oven and place the leeks cut side down on the melted butter. Use a pastry brush to brush the oil on top of the leeks. Cover the baking sheet loosely with foil and bake for about 25 minutes, until the bottom cut side turns golden.

Using a spatula, carefully turn the leeks over. Add the lemon juice, zest, and chicken stock to the baking sheet. Cover loosely and cook for another 15 minutes, or until very tender.

For additional caramelization, preheat the broiler. Uncover the leeks and place them under the broiler for about 1 minute, being careful not to burn them. Serve warm.

Prep Time: 10 minutes, plus
24 hours chilling time (marinate)
Cook Time: 40 minutes, plus
1 hour cooling time

Sweet and Sour Cipollini Onions

Cipollini are small, flat Italian onions that have a high sugar content, so they caramelize well. If you can't find them at your local market, you could substitute pearl onions. These make a nice side dish for the Pan-Grilled Pork Chops and Pineapples with Pineapple Rum Glaze (page 175) or an appetizer served alongside sliced meats like prosciutto and sopressata. Sliced, they would also be an excellent topping on a flatbread with arugula and Gorgonzola.

2 tablespoons olive oil

8 ounces (8 to 10) cipollini onions, peeled

¼ teaspoon kosher salt

⅓ cup red wine vinegar

¼ cup balsamic vinegar

1 tablespoon brown sugar

1 small garlic clove, minced

1 bay leaf

In a sauté pan over medium heat, add the oil to warm. Add the onions and salt and cook for 10 to 15 minutes, stirring occasionally to rotate, until golden brown on all sides. Set aside.

In a small saucepan over low heat, add red wine vinegar, balsamic vinegar, brown sugar, garlic, and bay leaf and cook while stirring until the sugar is dissolved.

Carefully transfer the onions to the saucepan, increase the heat to medium-high, and boil for about 5 minutes while stirring. Turn the heat down to low and simmer for about 20 minutes, until onions are just fork-tender.

Let the onions cool to room temperature in the liquid, about 1 hour. Serve warm or transfer to an airtight container and place in the refrigerator for 24 hours and up to 1 week.

Green Beans Amandine

There are some classics that never get old, and this is one of them. Frenching the bean is the extra step that opens up the surface area to be coated with butter and sherry vinegar and softens the bean just enough to contrast with the crunchy almonds. You can French or slice the beans using a knife or a bean slicer.

8 ounces green beans

1 tablespoon salted butter

1 teaspoon sherry or red wine vinegar

¼ cup Toasted Almonds (page 33)

Pinch of kosher salt

Pinch of freshly ground black pepper

Cook's Note: If using haricots verts, which are thin green beans, it would not be necessary to French or slice the beans. Just trim the stem ends and proceed with cooking.

To French cut larger green beans, use a knife to trim the stems and any tough ends with a diagonal cut, then slice the bean in half lengthwise. If you're using a bean slicer, trim the ends with the slicer, then pass each bean through the opening to slice them.

Prepare an ice bath by filling a large bowl with ice-cold water and ice cubes.

In a stockpot, bring 4 quarts of salted water to a rolling boil. Add the beans and cover the pot briefly until the water returns to a boil. Uncover the pot and cook for 2 to 5 minutes, until the beans are tender but crisp. Immediately drain the beans, rinse under cold water, and place into the ice bath. Drain and dry the beans; set aside.

In a skillet over medium-low heat, add the butter and heat until melted. Add the cooked beans and toss until coated and warm, 1 to 2 minutes. Add the sherry vinegar and toss to coat. Transfer to a serving dish. Sprinkle with toasted almonds and season with salt and pepper. Serve warm.

Stuffed Artichokes with Toasted Pine Nuts and Black Olives

This is a family recipe on my mom's (Italian) side that goes back a few generations, with each family member adding a tweak or extra ingredient. For us, it is synonymous with home, family, and holiday gatherings. Recipes like this one stick around for so many generations because they hit all the right senses in our memories. From their preparation to even the act of eating them, it is a very hands-on, family-style event. It's not just a recipe, it's a time-tested tradition ready to be started in your own home.

4 medium-size fresh globe artichokes

1¼ teaspoons kosher salt

3 tablespoons extra-virgin olive oil, plus more for coating leaves

2 garlic cloves, minced

2 tablespoons chopped flat-leaf parsley

1 tablespoon chopped basil

2 cups fresh Italian bread crumbs

⅓ cup toasted pine nuts

8 large pitted black olives, coarsely chopped

¼ teaspoon freshly ground black pepper

¾ cup chicken or vegetable stock

½ cup shredded mozzarella

¼ cup grated Parmesan cheese

To prepare the artichokes, use a large serrated knife to trim and discard about 1 inch off the top of each artichoke and trim the stems about ¾ inch above the base (cut evenly so the artichokes can stand upright). Using scissors, cut off and discard the pointed tips of each leaf. Gently spread out the leaves to expose the inner petals, which look like a flower bud with a purple or fuchsia tint. With a salad fork, begin to remove the "bud" from its outer edges by lifting up from underneath; discard. (You may need your fingers to assist in grabbing as much of the bud as possible.) With a spoon, scrape and scoop away the fuzzy center "choke," being careful not to damage the soft, flat disk underneath, which is the artichoke heart and most tender part of this dish. Rinse the hollow center with cold water to flush out any remaining choke, then pat dry. Drizzle the artichokes with olive oil and rub into the leaves to coat.

Fill a large pot with about 2 inches of water, cover, and bring to a boil. Place the prepared artichokes into the water, stem end up, and sprinkle generously with 1 teaspoon of the salt. Cover the pot again and simmer on medium-low heat for about 30 minutes. (You will know they are done when you can easily poke a fork into the artichoke from the base of the stem.)

While the artichokes are simmering, place a large skillet or sauté pan over medium heat. Add 2 tablespoons of the olive oil and heat until warm. Add the garlic and cook for 1 minute. Add the parsley and basil, sauté for 1 to 2 minutes, or until fragrant. Stir in the bread crumbs, pine nuts, olives, the remaining ¼ teaspoon of salt, and pepper, and continue to cook, stirring

CONTINUED

CONTINUED

Stuffed Artichokes with Toasted Pine Nuts and Black Olives

Cook's Notes: Try to choose artichokes that are heavy and firm. The leaves should be unblemished, tightly closed, and brittle. The base should be green.

How to eat the artichokes: Peel off one outer leaf at a time. Place the leaf in your mouth between your upper and lower teeth and pull slowly, allowing your teeth to scrape off the stuffing and softened base of the leaf. Discard what remains of the leaf after the soft part has been eaten. As you come to the center section of the artichoke, the leaves become tender and wholly edible. The center of the artichoke has extra stuffing, and just beneath that is the delicious soft artichoke heart. You will want to use your fork and knife to eat this section.

until toasted, about 2 minutes. Remove from the heat and drizzle with the ¼ cup of the chicken broth over the bread crumb mixture to moisten. Gently toss in the mozzarella and Parmesan until evenly distributed and set aside.

Line a plate with a few paper towels. Gently remove the softened artichokes from the water and transfer to the paper towels to drain and cool.

Preheat the oven to 375°F.

Stuff each center of the artichokes with about ¼ cup of the bread crumb mixture, starting from the outside leaves and working toward the middle. Continue to add the mixture between all the rows of leaves. Drizzle the remaining tablespoon of olive oil over the tops of the artichokes and transfer them to a baking dish. Pour the remaining ½ cup of stock into the bottom of the pan, cover with aluminum foil, and bake for 30 minutes, or until the center is fork tender. Remove the foil and bake uncovered for an additional 5 minutes.

Serve warm with an empty bowl on the side to receive the discarded artichoke leaves. (See Cook's Notes.)

If making ahead, cover the assembled baking dish with plastic wrap before the final bake and store it in the refrigerator for up to 2 days. To reheat, bake in a 375°F oven, covered with foil, for 45 minutes or until cooked through.

Roasted Brussels Sprouts with Crispy Shallots and Lemon Zest

When it comes to vegetable dishes, there is nothing better than roasted brussels sprouts, unless of course you happen to garnish them with crispy fried shallots and crushed toasted coriander seeds—and let's not forget the lemon zest and wedges. Overachiever? Perhaps, but don't judge me until you have sampled the sprouts.

1 pound brussels sprouts

½ teaspoon coriander seeds

2 tablespoons olive oil

¾ teaspoon kosher salt

Pinch of freshly ground black pepper

1½ teaspoons granulated sugar

⅓ cup canola oil

1 large shallot, thinly sliced

½ teaspoon lemon zest

½ lemon, cut into 4 wedges

Preheat the oven to 425°F. Line a rimmed baking sheet with parchment paper.

Trim any browned stem ends of the Brussels sprouts, and remove any loose leaves. Cut them in half lengthwise (or cut in quarters, if bigger than 2 inches wide).

In a small skillet over medium heat, cook the coriander seeds, shaking the pan occasionally, until lightly toasted and fragrant, about 3 minutes. Let cool slightly, then use the back of a cast-iron skillet or a mortar and pestle to coarsely crush the seeds. Set aside.

Add the brussels sprouts to a large mixing bowl, drizzle with olive oil, sprinkle with ½ teaspoon of the salt, pepper, and sugar, and toss to combine.

Arrange the brussels sprouts in a single layer on the prepared baking sheet. Transfer to the oven and roast for about 25 minutes, stirring halfway through, until evenly caramelized.

Meanwhile, in a large cast-iron skillet over medium heat, add the canola oil and heat until it starts to shimmer. Add the shallot slices in a single layer and cook for about 2 minutes, until the bubbling starts to slow down. Turn the heat down to low and cook for 3 to 5 more minutes, stirring occasionally, until golden brown. Use a slotted spoon to remove the shallot slices and transfer them to a paper towel–lined plate to drain. Season with the remaining ¼ teaspoon of salt and another pinch of pepper. Let cool slightly. (Discard the oil and any shallot pieces that look blackened.)

Transfer the roasted sprouts to a serving dish. Top with the crispy shallots. Sprinkle with the lemon zest and crushed coriander. Squeeze the lemon wedges over the sprouts before serving.

Roasted Delicata Squash with Tahini Sauce and Toasted Pepitas

Delicata squash is a Japanese winter squash with a shell that is tender and edible when cooked. Mâche greens are salad greens that have small, dark, velvety leaves with a rich, sweet flavor, similar to hazelnuts. Mâche is available throughout the year in gourmet produce shops. Select bunches that are thick and have fresh, brightly colored leaves. If you are unable to find mâche greens, you can substitute freshly cut spinach or baby arugula, or, for a pleasant spicy contrast, try watercress greens.

Squash

Nonstick vegetable spray

1 delicata squash, cut crosswise into ½-inch-thick rounds

2 tablespoons salted butter, melted

Pepitas

1 teaspoon salted butter

2 tablespoons raw pepitas

Pinch of smoked paprika

Pinch of kosher salt

Tahini Sauce

2 tablespoons tahini (with oil, or add 1 teaspoon olive oil)

2 tablespoons water

1 tablespoon fresh lemon juice

1 small garlic clove, minced

Pinch of kosher salt

Black pepper

1 cup mâche or watercress greens

Flaky sea salt

Freshly ground black pepper

To make the squash: Preheat the oven to 400°F. Line a baking sheet with aluminum foil and spray lightly with nonstick spray.

Place the squash slices in a single layer on the prepared baking sheet, drizzle with the melted butter, and roast for about 30 minutes, turning halfway through, until tender all the way through and golden brown in places. Let cool slightly and then use a fork to pull out and discard seeds.

To toast the pepitas: In a skillet over medium heat, melt the butter. Add the seeds and sprinkle with paprika and kosher salt, stirring to coat evenly. Continue to cook while shaking the pan and stirring often until golden brown and slightly puffed, 5 to 7 minutes. Transfer to a plate to cool.

To make the tahini sauce: In a small bowl, whisk together the tahini, water, lemon juice, garlic, and salt until smooth. Set aside.

To assemble, plate the roasted squash over a bed of mâche greens and drizzle with the tahini sauce. Sprinkle with the toasted pepitas and season with flaky sea salt and freshly ground black pepper to taste.

Celery Root and Parsnip Gratin

Parsnips and celery root (or celeriac) are wonderful candidates for a root vegetable gratin, and arguably make for a lighter, earthier, and more refreshing gratin than classic potatoes do. It would make a wonderful accompaniment to hearty dishes around the holidays. They do tend to render more liquid than potatoes, so it helps to start them on the stovetop to let some steam cook off and to allow the starches to thicken the cream. They also need a little extra resting time after being cooked. Any residual liquid in the dish can be spooned over the top of the gratin when serving.

½ celery root

3 tablespoons salted butter

2 garlic cloves, smashed

1 cup heavy cream

¼ cup vegetable stock

2 sprigs thyme, plus 1 sprig for garnish (optional)

1 bay leaf

1 large parsnip, peeled and cut crosswise into ⅛- to ¼-inch-thick slices

½ teaspoon kosher salt

¼ teaspoon freshly ground black pepper

Pinch of nutmeg

½ cup grated Gruyère

½ cup grated Parmesan cheese

To prepare the celery root, use a sharp knife to remove the ends, taking a small slice off the top and more off the bottom root side until only the white insides are visible. Lay the flat side down and use a sharp knife to remove the thick skin until no brown parts remain. Cut the root into quarters lengthwise. Using a mandoline or very sharp knife, cut each quarter crosswise into thin slices (about ⅛ to ¼ inch thick).

Preheat the oven to 450°F. Grease a baking dish or gratin dish with 1 tablespoon of the butter and set it on a rimmed baking sheet. Rub the baking dish with the smashed garlic, reserving the garlic when finished.

In a saucepan over medium-high heat, add the cream, stock, the reserved garlic, thyme, and bay leaf, stirring to combine, and bring to a simmer.

Add the slices of celery root and parsnip and gently stir to combine. Add salt, pepper, and nutmeg. Let simmer for about 10 minutes until just tender.

Remove the garlic, bay leaf, and thyme. Transfer the vegetables and the cream mixture to the prepared dish, using a spatula to lay the slices down flat and evenly distribute them. Cover with the Gruyère and Parmesan and sprinkle with thin shavings of the remaining 2 tablespoons of butter. Garnish with a fresh sprig of thyme, if desired.

Bake for about 30 minutes, until golden and bubbling and the vegetables are tender. Remove and let stand for 10 to 15 minutes before serving to allow the vegetables to absorb some of the excess liquid.

Cheddar Spoon Bread with Lime and Pink Peppercorns

A traditional Southern side dish, this falls somewhere between a corn casserole and a soufflé. The whole corn kernels add a layer of texture to an otherwise light, creamy side dish. A little bit of lime juice and zest brightens the flavors and enhances the sweetness of the corn. The smoked sea salt and pink peppercorns, while not essential to the recipe, are a really nice finishing touch.

2 tablespoons salted butter, plus more for coating the ramekins

1½ cups milk

1 teaspoon smoked sea salt

1 teaspoon freshly ground pink peppercorns

½ cup fine cornmeal

2 tablespoons cream cheese

1 tablespoon fresh lime juice

1 teaspoon lime zest

½ teaspoon baking powder

⅔ cup shredded sharp Cheddar cheese

2 or 3 dashes hot sauce

2 eggs, separated

2 teaspoons granulated sugar

½ cup cooked corn kernels

Cook's Note: It is best to have all the ingredients measured and ready at room temperature before starting.

Preheat the oven to 375°F. Using 1 tablespoon of the butter, coat the bottoms only of four 6-ounce ramekins. Place on a baking sheet and set aside.

In a saucepan over medium heat, heat 1 cup of the milk, ½ teaspoon of the smoked salt, and ½ teaspoon of the pink peppercorns to a simmer. Slowly add the cornmeal, whisking continuously, and cook until the mixture starts to thicken, about 2 minutes. Remove from the heat and add in the cream cheese, the remaining 1 tablespoon of butter, lime juice, ½ teaspoon of the lime zest, baking powder, cheese, and hot sauce. Whisk until well-incorporated.

In a small bowl, whisk the egg yolks into the remaining ½ cup of milk, then whisk into the cornmeal batter. Set aside.

In a stand mixer fitted with the whisk attachment on medium-high, beat the egg whites until soft peaks form. Turn the mixer to low, add the sugar, then increase the speed and whip until peaks become stiff and have a slight sheen. Using a spatula, gently fold about one-quarter of the whipped egg whites into the batter to loosen it, then fold in the remainder of the egg whites until only faint streaks of white remain. Fold in the whole corn kernels until just incorporated.

Evenly divide the batter among the prepared ramekins and fill to just below the top rim. Using a butter knife, draw a circle around the top inside edge of the mixture to help the spoon bread rise.

Bake for about 20 minutes, until puffed, golden, and slightly jiggly in the center. Serve immediately, garnished with the remaining smoked salt, pink peppercorns, and lime zest.

Crispy Duck Fat Potatoes with Horseradish Crème Fraîche

I am certain that crispy duck fat potatoes would be at the top of my request list for my last meal (I am also certain it would be a very lengthy list). Duck fat is compared to liquid gold in the fat department because it imparts wonderful flavor and has a relatively high smoking point. I shake the pan to rough up the potatoes not because I am a potato bully but to create cracks and pockets that will become infused with flavor and add crispness. Along with many words of wisdom imparted at my last request meal, I may be quoted as saying, "And bring an extra side of horseradish crème fraîche."

¼ cup crème fraîche

2 tablespoons prepared horseradish

2 tablespoons heavy cream

1 tablespoon apple cider vinegar

1 tablespoon plus ½ teaspoon kosher salt

½ teaspoon baking soda

1½ pounds Yukon gold potatoes, peeled and halved

2 tablespoons duck fat

1 garlic clove, minced

¼ teaspoon freshly ground black pepper

Pinch of smoked paprika

Cook's Note: The size of a medium Yukon gold potato can vary greatly. You want about 1½-inch chunks for this recipe, so if the potatoes are on the large side, you may need to cut them into quarters instead of halves.

Stir together the crème fraîche, horseradish, and heavy cream until well combined. Cover and chill until ready to use.

Preheat the oven to 475°F.

In a large saucepan, bring 2 quarts of water to a boil. Add the vinegar, 1 tablespoon of the salt, and baking soda. Add the potatoes and boil for about 10 minutes, until just fork-tender. Turn off the heat, drain the potatoes, then return them to the empty warm stockpot. Shake the pot for 1 to 3 minutes until the exterior of the potatoes have a rugged, gummy appearance.

Meanwhile, in a sauté pan over medium-low heat, melt the duck fat with the garlic until fragrant, being careful not to burn the garlic. Strain the duck fat into the pot of cooked potatoes and toss to coat. Discard the garlic. Transfer the potatoes to a rimmed baking sheet and spread them out into a single layer. Sprinkle with the remaining ½ teaspoon salt, the pepper, and smoked paprika.

Bake until the potatoes are crispy and a rich golden brown, 30 to 40 minutes, stirring and turning occasionally.

Serve warm with horseradish crème fraîche on the side.

Prep Time: 10 minutes, plus a
minimum of 1 hour chilling time
Cook Time: 30 minutes

Red Potato Salad with Smoked Bacon and Chives

A little creamy, a little vinegary, this potato salad is just trying to win everyone's heart.

2 pounds baby red potatoes, halved (or quartered depending on size)

2½ teaspoons kosher salt, plus more as needed

3 tablespoons apple cider vinegar

4 slices hickory smoked bacon

¼ cup mayonnaise

3 tablespoons minced red onion

1 tablespoon prepared horseradish

1 tablespoon pickle juice

1 teaspoon granulated sugar

¼ teaspoon freshly ground black pepper, plus more as needed

2 tablespoons diced chives

Add the potatoes to a large saucepan and add enough water to cover the potatoes. Add 2 teaspoons of the salt and 1 tablespoon of the vinegar and bring to a boil over medium-high heat. Cook the potatoes until they are tender, about 15 minutes. Drain the potatoes in a colander and transfer them to a rimmed baking sheet. Drizzle with the remaining 2 tablespoons vinegar, and let cool completely.

In a cast-iron skillet, place the bacon slices side by side. Set the skillet over medium-low heat and cook until the bacon has rendered its fat and the slices can be easily released from the pan with tongs. Flip the bacon slices over and cook until evenly browned and crispy on both sides, flipping and turning as needed. The whole process should take 8 to 10 minutes. Transfer to paper towels to drain and blot to remove excess fat. Cut the bacon into ½-inch pieces and set aside.

In a serving bowl, combine the mayonnaise, red onion, horseradish, pickle juice, sugar, the remaining ½ teaspoon of salt, and the pepper. Add the potatoes, bacon, and chives and toss. Season to taste with additional salt and pepper. Cover and refrigerate for at least 1 hour or up to 3 days. Serve cold.

MAKES 2 SERVINGS

Prep Time: 15 minutes
Cook Time: 45 minutes

Autumn Harvest Farro Salad with Persimmons

This grain salad is reminiscent of the flavors and colors of fall. It is a healthy, satisfying, and interesting combination of ingredients with a light dressing that brings it all together. It's also a great vegan option if you eliminate the goat cheese. Ripe persimmons could be substituted with pears or even roasted winter squash, such as butternut or delicata (see page 129).

1½ cups water

1 teaspoon kosher salt

½ cup farro

¼ cup raw chopped walnuts

⅓ cup canola oil (or safflower oil)

1½ tablespoons white balsamic vinegar or champagne vinegar

1 teaspoon honey

1 teaspoon minced shallot (optional)

2 teaspoons tahini

1 small head radicchio, trimmed, quartered, cored, and cut crosswise into 1-inch-wide strips

¼ cup dried cranberries, coarsely chopped

2 Fuyu persimmons, peeled, cored, and cut into wedges (or rounds)

1 ounce goat cheese, crumbled

¼ teaspoon coarse sea salt

Pinch of freshly ground black pepper

In a saucepan over high heat, bring the water and kosher salt to a boil. Add the farro, stir, and cook, uncovered over low heat for 30 to 45 minutes, until just tender. Drain and set aside to cool.

In a heavy skillet over medium heat, add the walnuts and cook, stirring frequently, until lightly toasted and fragrant, 2 to 3 minutes.

In a small container that can be sealed with a lid, add the canola oil, balsamic vinegar, honey, shallot (if using), and tahini. Shake until emulsified.

In a large bowl, toss together the farro, radicchio, walnuts, and cranberries. Pour on the vinaigrette and toss to coat. Top with the persimmons and small dollops of goat cheese. Season with sea salt and pepper.

Chilled Pasta Salad with Summer Squash and Tomatoes

To serve this pasta salad, hastily dump it into a big storage container, throw it into a bag packed for a picnic (don't forget the plates, forks, napkins, and beverages of choice), and head out the door with your plus-one. Meeting up with friends? The cold-pressed eggplant sandwiches (page 88) would make an excellent addition to the picnic spread.

Dressing

2 tablespoons red wine vinegar

1 tablespoon Dijon mustard

2 teaspoons fresh Meyer lemon juice

1 teaspoon granulated sugar

½ teaspoon kosher salt

1 small garlic clove, minced

¼ cup canola or safflower oil

¼ cup extra-virgin olive oil

Salad

8 ounces dry rotini or fusilli pasta

3 tablespoons olive oil

4 summer squash (such as yellow or zucchini), cut into quarters lengthwise, then into ½-inch-thick slices

4 ounces salami, cut into ¼-inch cubes

4 ounces fresh mozzarella (pearls or bocconcini)

1½ cups cherry tomatoes, halved

⅓ cup chopped pitted kalamata olives

1 tablespoon finely chopped basil

2 teaspoons finely chopped flat-leaf parsley

Freshly ground black pepper

To make the dressing: In a small bowl, whisk together the vinegar, mustard, lemon juice, sugar, salt, and garlic. Drizzle in the canola and olive oils in a steady stream while whisking until emulsified. Set aside until ready to use.

To make the salad: Bring a large pot of salted water to a boil and cook the pasta al dente, according to the package directions. Drain and toss with 1 tablespoon of the olive oil. Transfer to a rimmed baking sheet to let cool.

In a large sauté pan over medium high heat, heat the remaining 2 tablespoons olive oil until hot. Add the zucchini and squash and sauté, stirring occasionally, until softened and starting to turn a light golden brown, about 7 minutes. Set aside to cool.

In a large bowl, add the pasta, zucchini, squash, salami, mozzarella, tomatoes, olives, basil, and parsley and toss to combine. Pour in the vinaigrette and toss to coat. Season with salt and pepper. Cover and refrigerate to let the flavors marinate for at least 2 hours or overnight.

Cook's Notes: If you like the idea of the cubed salami, try ordering ¼ to ½ pound of salami at your favorite deli or grocery store deli counter and ask if they could cut the salami into a single thick slice.

Mains

Pizza with Caramelized Figs, Baby Arugula, and Smoked Mozzarella

You can make amazing pizza at home with this recipe. Please give the pizza dough recipe (page 42) a try (it's delicious), or use store-bought dough if you are short on time. You might even be able to buy some dough from your favorite pizza shop—just ask. If you're brand new at making pizza at home, try making a pizza with a basic marinara sauce and fresh mozzarella as your first test batch. Don't give up if something doesn't go as expected the first time. Then when figs are in season, you can give this one a shot.

Homemade Pizza Dough (page 42) or 1 pound store-bought pizza dough

2 teaspoons honey

1 teaspoon salted butter

4 small ripe fresh figs, halved or quartered

1 tablespoon olive oil

¾ cup shredded smoked mozzarella

1 small shallot, thinly sliced

¼ teaspoon apple cider vinegar

⅓ cup baby arugula

Pinch of kosher salt

Pinch of freshly ground black pepper

2½ tablespoons crème fraîche

1 teaspoon finely crushed shelled pistachios

Pinch of flaky sea salt

See the instructions for making and shaping the pizza dough on page 42, including preheating the oven with the pizza stone.

In a large skillet over medium heat, stir together the honey and butter and cook until warm and runny. Add the figs, cut side down, and cook until slightly caramelized, about 5 minutes. Set aside.

Using a pastry brush, lightly coat the pizza dough with 2 teaspoons of the olive oil in a few light strokes. Sprinkle the dough with the mozzarella, leaving a ½-inch border around the edge. Top with the shallot.

Using the pizza peel (see Cook's Notes, page 41), slide the pizza dough onto the pizza stone. Bake until the crust is browned and crispy, about 8 minutes, depending on your oven temperature and the thickness of the crust.

While the pizza bakes, whisk together the remaining 1 teaspoon of olive oil and apple cider vinegar until blended. In a bowl, add the arugula and sprinkle with kosher salt and pepper. Drizzle with the oil and vinegar mixture and toss to coat. Set aside.

When the pizza is done baking, use the pizza peel to remove the pizza from the oven by sliding the peel under the pizza and transferring onto a wire rack to cool for about 3 minutes. Top with the dressed arugula and caramelized figs. Place a few dollops of crème fraîche on top. Sprinkle with pistachios and flaky sea salt. Cut into slices and serve right away.

Cook's Notes: I like the look of figs with their stems on. They act as nice little handles when you need to transfer them during cooking processes, but you could trim them before placing the figs on the pizza if you prefer.

Smoky Mac and Cheese with Carolina Candied Bacon

We don't own a smoker since my dad and brother-in-law are our family's barbecue pitmasters, so to speak—they have that department more than covered. When I get a smoking craving (for barbecue, that is), this mac and cheese will be here as my "patch." It is infused with smoky flavors from the lightly toasted roux, melty smoked Cheddar cheese and Gouda, and a bread-crumb topping toasted up with smoked paprika. The icing on the cake is a bacon topping, candied with barbecue sauce and malt vinegar. I hope this will help hold you over until your next barbecue, too.

Bread-Crumb Topping

2 tablespoons mayonnaise

¼ cup grated Parmesan cheese

¼ teaspoon smoked paprika

1 or 2 slices sourdough bread, 1 inch thick

Carolina Candied Bacon

1 tablespoon barbecue sauce

1 tablespoon malt vinegar

1 teaspoon brown sugar

2 slices thick-cut bacon

Pasta

¼ cup salted butter, plus 1 tablespoon for greasing the pan

¼ cup all-purpose flour

2½ cups whole milk

Kosher salt

¼ teaspoon freshly ground black pepper

To make the bread-crumb topping: Preheat the oven to 400°F. In a small bowl, stir together the mayonnaise, Parmesan, and smoked paprika until combined. Spread the mayonnaise mixture onto both sides of the bread slices and place them on a baking sheet. Bake for about 10 minutes, flipping halfway through, until lightly toasted on both sides. Let the bread cool before transferring it to the bowl of a food processor, breaking it into smaller pieces as needed to fit. Pulse until the mixture resembles fine to coarse crumbs. Use immediately or store in an airtight container in the refrigerator for up to 3 days.

To make the candied bacon: Preheat the oven to 400°F. Line a rimmed baking sheet with parchment paper. In a small bowl, mix together the barbecue sauce, malt vinegar, and brown sugar. Using a pastry brush, generously coat both sides of the bacon slices with the barbecue sauce mixture. Transfer to the oven and bake for about 12 minutes, flipping halfway through, until just starting to caramelize but not yet crisp. Drain on a paper towel–lined plate. Cut the bacon crosswise into ¼-inch strips. Set aside.

To make the pasta: Preheat the oven to 375°F. Grease a 1½- to 2-quart baking dish with 1 tablespoon of the butter.

In a large heavy saucepan or Dutch oven over medium heat, melt the remaining butter. Add the flour and whisk constantly until it just starts to turn a light golden brown and has a nutty aroma, about 6 minutes. Turn down the heat to medium-low, and slowly add the milk, whisking constantly until smooth, and continue to cook while stirring until thickened, about 15 minutes.

CONTINUED

CONTINUED

Smoky Mac and Cheese with Carolina Candied Bacon

¼ teaspoon dry mustard

¼ teaspoon smoked paprika

Pinch of nutmeg

6 ounces smoked
Cheddar, grated

3 ounces smoked
Gouda, grated

3 ounces Comté, grated

8 ounces dry large
elbow macaroni

Add ¼ teaspoon salt, the pepper, mustard powder, smoked paprika, nutmeg, and cheeses and stir until smooth and well combined.

Bring a large pot of salted water to a boil. Cook the pasta according to the package directions for al dente; drain well and pour the pasta into the cheese mixture. Stir well to combine before transferring it to the baking dish.

Sprinkle the bread crumbs and bacon over the macaroni and cheese. Cover with aluminum foil and bake for about 20 minutes, until bubbling hot. Remove the foil and return to the oven to bake for an additional 10 minutes, or until the toppings look golden brown and crispy.

To make ahead, add the macaroni and cheese to the baking dish, cover tightly with plastic wrap, and store in the refrigerator for up to 2 days. When ready to cook, sprinkle the bread crumbs and bacon over the top, cover with aluminum foil and bake for about 45 minutes, until warmed through.

Bourbon Risotto with Pan-Fried Mushrooms

This risotto is cooked with bourbon instead of white wine or vermouth, a discovery my sister-in-law made when preparing risotto for a crowd while on vacation with friends, and bourbon was the only spirit at her disposal. Apparently, the smell of the bourbon cooking piqued the interest of the hungry houseguests, and everyone raved that it was the best risotto they had ever eaten. The combination of dry red wine and bourbon creates depth and complements the earthy unique flavors that you get from fresh mushrooms.

A creamy texture is key and can be achieved from the rice itself. But for a little "more is more," I've followed the lead of some very reputable chefs who fold in whipped cream to add a rich flavor with a light and creamy texture. Here I use whipped crème fraîche for a bright and interesting tang.

Pan-Fried Mushrooms

8 ounces assorted fresh mushrooms (any combination of chanterelle, maitake, oyster, shiitake, cremini, baby bella, or others)

2 tablespoons extra-virgin olive oil

2 teaspoons chopped flat-leaf parsley

¼ teaspoon chopped thyme

Mushroom Pan Sauce

2 tablespoons salted butter

1 small garlic clove, minced

¼ cup pan-fried mushrooms

¼ teaspoon kosher salt

¼ teaspoon freshly ground black pepper

Pinch of smoked paprika

½ cup dry red wine

To make the pan-fried mushrooms: Rub off any dirt from the dry, fresh mushrooms with a damp paper towel. Cut the mushrooms into 1-inch pieces, but tear the chanterelles in half. Heat a large nonstick skillet over medium-high heat until hot and add 1 tablespoon of the oil. When the oil starts to shimmer, add the mushrooms, working in batches, if necessary, so as not to crowd the pan. Cook the mushrooms, tossing occasionally, until well browned on all sides and most of the residual moisture has evaporated, 5 to 8 minutes. Stir in the parsley and thyme. Transfer all but ¼ cup of the mushrooms to a plate, cover the plate loosely with aluminum foil, and set it aside.

To make the mushroom pan sauce: Add 1 tablespoon of the butter and the garlic to the skillet of reserved mushrooms, then season with the salt, pepper, and paprika. Cook while stirring over medium-high heat until fragrant. Add the wine and cook until it is reduced by half, 3 to 5 minutes. Turn off the heat and stir in the remaining tablespoon of butter. Set aside.

To make the risotto: In a saucepan over medium-high heat, bring the broth to a simmer. Turn the heat down to low.

In a large Dutch oven over medium heat, melt the butter. Add the onion and cook, stirring occasionally, until softened, about 5 minutes.

CONTINUED

CONTINUED

Bourbon Risotto with Pan-Fried Mushrooms

Bourbon Risotto

3 to 4½ cups mushroom broth (or vegetable broth)

2 tablespoons salted butter

1 small onion, chopped

1 cup arborio or carnaroli rice

2½ tablespoons bourbon

1½ tablespoons dry red wine

Kosher salt and freshly ground black pepper

3 tablespoons crème fraîche, whipped to soft peaks

2 tablespoons shaved Parmesan cheese, preferably Parmigiano-Reggiano

Add the rice and cook, stirring with a wooden spoon, about 3 minutes. Add the bourbon and red wine, stirring constantly. Increase the heat to medium-high and continue to cook, while stirring continually, until all of the liquid is absorbed by the rice. Add ½ teaspoon of salt.

Using a ladle, add one ladleful of broth at a time to the rice mixture, stirring after each addition. Add just enough broth to just keep the rice hydrated and continue to stir and scrape the pan as the broth evaporates in order to prevent sticking. When the broth is almost fully absorbed, add another ladleful of broth. The mixture should never be too dry.

Continue to cook and gradually add the broth, stirring continually and adjusting the heat as needed to maintain a gentle simmer, until the rice is cooked but still al dente. This could be about 18 minutes from the first addition of broth or up to 30 minutes. You may not need all of the broth, so it is important to taste the rice frequently to determine its doneness.

Once the rice is cooked to al dente, remove the pan from the heat. If the risotto looks too thick, add a tablespoon or two of the warm broth. Season with additional salt and pepper. Fold in the whipped crème fraîche.

Ladle the risotto into two shallow bowls. Top with the pan-fried mushrooms and sprinkle with Parmesan. Spoon a small amount of warm mushroom pan sauce over the mushrooms and around the risotto.

Cole's Carbonara

Spaghetti carbonara is a go-to dinner for us because the ingredients are (mostly) always stocked in our household. This recipe is Cole's specialty and, true to his nature, is not a purist carbonara. The addition of peas, red bell pepper, shallots, and tomatoes are non-traditional, but they give this dish a subtle twist with a little brightness in flavor and color. What is traditional is the creamy and silky texture of the pasta. This is a quick-moving recipe, so even Cole (and we suggest you, too) has learned to embrace a mise en place approach here.

2 eggs plus 1 egg yolk, lightly beaten

⅓ cup finely grated Parmesan cheese, preferably Parmigiano-Reggiano, plus 2 tablespoons for serving

Kosher salt

2 tablespoons extra-virgin olive oil

1 large garlic clove, quartered

½ large red bell pepper, seeded and finely diced

½ teaspoon kosher salt, plus more as needed

6 strips thick-cut bacon, cut crosswise into ½-inch pieces

1 shallot, sliced

8 ounces dry spaghetti pasta

½ cup frozen peas

¾ cup grape tomatoes or small cherry tomatoes

2 tablespoons salted butter

Freshly ground black pepper

Mix together the eggs and ⅓ cup of the Parmesan cheese. Set aside.

Bring a large pot of salted water to a boil.

In a large skillet over medium heat, warm the oil until hot. Add the garlic and sauté for about 30 seconds, until golden and fragrant. Remove the garlic and discard. Add the bell pepper and season with the salt. Cook for about 3 minutes, stirring occasionally, until softened and the pepper has an orange tint. Add the bacon and cook, stirring occasionally, for 5 to 7 minutes, until the bacon is fully cooked but not crispy. Add the shallot and continue to cook and stir for 3 minutes, or until tender.

While the shallot cooks, add the pasta to the boiling water. Cook the pasta according to the package directions, about 9 minutes, until just shy of al dente. During the final minute of cooking the pasta, add the peas to the pasta pot with a quick stir. Reserve a ladleful of the pasta cooking water before draining the pasta and peas thoroughly.

While the pasta is cooking, add the tomatoes to the skillet of bacon, and cook, stirring occasionally, over medium-high heat for 3 to 5 minutes, until the skins are slightly shriveled and just bursting. Turn off the heat.

Add the cooked pasta and peas to the bacon in the skillet. Add the butter and 2 tablespoons of the reserved pasta water, and gently stir to combine. Add the egg mixture and toss quickly and thoroughly until well combined but still glossy; you do not want the egg to cook. You may need to add an additional tablespoon of the pasta water if pasta is sticking together.

Transfer the carbonara to pasta bowls and season with additional salt and a good amount of freshly ground black pepper. Sprinkle with the remaining 2 tablespoons Parmesan. Serve immediately.

Prep Time: 15 minutes, plus
30 minutes inactive time
Cook Time: 1 hour, 15 minutes

Beef Stroganoff

While a traditional beef stroganoff uses beef sirloin steak cut into strips, this version gets upgraded with beef tenderloin filet. Let it be the star of the dish by plating it right on top, instead of covering it with the gravy—a perfect hearty dinner for two.

2 (4-ounce) beef tenderloin filet steaks, at room temperature

2 tablespoons salted butter

6 ounces pearl onions, peeled (fresh or frozen)

6 ounces baby bella mushrooms, stemmed and quartered

2 small whole garlic cloves

A few sprigs of thyme

1 cup chicken stock

1 cup dry white wine

2½ tablespoons sour cream (or crème fraîche), at room temperature

3 tablespoons Worcestershire sauce

¼ teaspoon dry mustard

¼ teaspoon coarse sea salt

¼ teaspoon freshly ground black pepper, plus more as needed

1 tablespoon avocado oil (or grapeseed oil)

6 ounces extra-wide egg noodles

2 tablespoons chopped flat-leaf parsley, for garnish

Preheat the oven to 400°F.

In a large sauté pan over medium heat, melt the butter and add the pearl onions. Cook, stirring occasionally, until fork-tender and lightly browned, about 15 minutes. Add 1 to 2 tablespoons of water if the onions start to dry out and stick to the pan. Add the mushrooms, garlic, and thyme and cook while stirring for about 10 minutes, until the mushrooms are golden brown. Turn off the heat and set aside.

In a small saucepan over medium-high heat, bring the chicken stock and white wine to a boil. Let simmer, uncovered, for about 20 minutes, until reduced by half.

In a bowl, whisk together the sour cream, Worcestershire, and dry mustard. While whisking, gradually add the warm broth reduction to the sour cream mixture. Pour the creamy broth into the sauté pan with the mushrooms and onions and set over low heat, stirring occasionally, to keep warm until serving.

Bring a large pot of salted water to a boil.

Generously season both sides of the steaks with the sea salt and pepper right before cooking.

Preheat a large cast-iron skillet over medium-high heat until hot. Sear the steaks for about 2 minutes, without moving, until browned. Add the avocado oil to the skillet and carefully turn the steaks over and cook for another 2 minutes on the other side until browned. Transfer the skillet with the steaks to the oven. Cook for about 10 minutes, or until the internal temperature is 130°F for medium rare or the desired level of doneness. Let rest under tented aluminum foil for 5 to 10 minutes.

Meanwhile, cook the noodles in the boiling water according to the package directions. Drain.

Slice the beef against the grain into ¼-inch-thick slices.

Distribute the noodles onto two rimmed plates or low bowls. Spoon the gravy, mushrooms, and onions over the noodles and top with the sliced steak. Garnish with the parsley and season with additional pepper to taste.

Miso Butter Scallops with Watercress and Cucumber Salad

Scallops are a popular entrée in many fine-dining establishments, but there are so many reasons you should try your hand at this recipe at home. Scallops are surprisingly quick and simple to prepare and are impressive for a special evening or event. The miso butter adds a rich, nutty umami flavor to the naturally sweet scallop.

Salad

1½ tablespoons extra-virgin olive oil

1 tablespoon rice vinegar

Pinch of flaky sea salt

2 cups watercress greens

½ English cucumber, thinly sliced

Scallops

2 tablespoons unsalted butter, at room temperature

1½ teaspoons white miso

Pinch of cayenne pepper

½ pound dry sea scallops, at room temperature or with a slight chill

1 tablespoon avocado oil (or safflower oil)

Pinch of flaky sea salt

Pinch of freshly ground black pepper

Cook's Notes: Dry scallops are fresh scallops that have not been chemically treated to retain moisture. Look for scallops that have a fleshy, translucent white or off-white color. Avoid "wet" scallops, which are pale, milky white and often sitting in a pool of liquid.

To make the salad: Whisk together the oil, vinegar, and sea salt until well blended and emulsified. In a large bowl, add the watercress and cucumber. Pour in the vinaigrette and gently toss until evenly distributed and lightly coated. Set aside.

To make the scallops: In a small bowl, add the butter, miso, and cayenne pepper and mix until well blended. Set aside.

To prepare the scallops, pull off and discard the small muscle foot attached to the side of the scallop, if present. Rinse the scallops under cold water, then place on paper towels, and pat until completely dry.

Heat a large stainless steel sauté pan or skillet over medium-high heat until very hot. Add the avocado oil and heat until the surface of the oil glistens. Season the scallops with sea salt and pepper just before adding them to the pan.

Carefully place the scallops, flat side down, in the skillet, working in clockwise order, and allowing space between each scallop. (They should instantly sizzle when they touch the pan.) Cook without moving for about 2 minutes, or until a deep golden brown sear is visible on the scallops' edges. Do not flip the scallops until there is a fully developed golden crust on the first side (this can be your presentation side).

Using a small metal spatula or spoon, flip over each scallop in the same order they were placed into the pan and cook for another 1 to 2 minutes. You should be able to see a golden sear that goes partially up the side of the scallops, but the center should still be slightly translucent. Turn off the heat and transfer the scallops to a paper towel–lined plate to drain briefly. Add the miso butter to the skillet to melt.

Plate the scallops, drizzle with the warm miso butter, and serve with the prepared salad.

Prep Time: 35 minutes,
plus 20 minutes inactive time
Cook Time: 15 minutes

Spicy Shrimp Tacos with Mexican-Style Slaw

Growing up, tacos were a hard-shell vehicle for seasoned ground meat, shredded cheese, and iceberg lettuce. I actually loved it at the time. I didn't really know it could be any different. But boy am I glad I met this Californian husband of mine, who introduced me to a world of tacos and burritos and enchiladas (see page 164) that I had never seen the likes of in any yellow box. These are one of his latest specialties. Not unlike his mom, he keeps it loose in the kitchen and makes a lovely mess when he cooks. I coaxed this recipe out of him, questioning him at every pan shake and extra pinch or dash.

Radishes

¼ cup red wine vinegar

1 small garlic clove, smashed

¼ teaspoon kosher salt

¼ teaspoon agave nectar

3 radishes, trimmed and julienned

Pico de Gallo

1 plum tomato, seeded and chopped

2 tablespoons finely chopped red onion

1½ tablespoons chopped cilantro, plus more for garnish

2 teaspoons freshly squeezed lime juice

Pinch of kosher salt

Slaw

1 tablespoon mayonnaise

½ teaspoon lime zest

¼ teaspoon kosher salt

To make the radishes: In a small bowl, whisk to combine the vinegar, garlic, salt, and agave nectar. Add the radishes, toss to coat, and let sit for at least 15 minutes to marinate.

To make the pico de gallo: Toss together the tomato, red onion, cilantro, lime juice, and salt. Set aside until ready to use.

To make the slaw: In a bowl, place 1 teaspoon of the pickling liquid from the radishes. Then add the mayonnaise, lime zest, salt, cayenne, chipotle pepper, and black pepper and whisk to combine. Add the cabbage and avocado, and toss to coat. Set aside.

Once the radishes have marinated for about 15 minutes, remove radishes from liquid with a slotted spoon and place on paper towels briefly to drain before transferring to a small bowl. Set aside.

To make the shrimp filling: Put the frozen shrimp in a colander and rinse with cold water for about 5 minutes, or until thawed. Pat dry with paper towels.

In a large skillet over medium-high heat, melt the butter until sizzling. Add the shrimp, garlic, and agave nectar, stirring to combine. Sprinkle with the salt, chipotle pepper, and cumin and stir to blend. Continue to cook while shaking the pan occasionally to stir and flip, until the shrimp are just barely translucent, 2 to 3 minutes. Add the pico de gallo and continue cooking until the shrimp are just opaque, about 1 additional minute.

CONTINUED

CONTINUED

Spicy Shrimp Tacos with Mexican-Style Slaw

Pinch of cayenne pepper

Pinch of chipotle pepper

Pinch of freshly ground black pepper

1 cup thinly shredded napa cabbage

½ small ripe avocado, cut into small ¼-inch cubes

Shrimp Filling

8 ounces peeled, deveined frozen extra-large shrimp (26 to 30 per pound)

1 tablespoon salted butter

2 small garlic cloves, minced

½ tablespoon agave nectar

¼ teaspoon kosher salt

¼ teaspoon chipotle pepper

¼ teaspoon ground cumin

Tortillas

1 teaspoon olive oil

6 (4-inch) corn tortillas, or 4 (6-inch) corn tortillas

¼ cup shredded Monterey Jack cheese

3 tablespoons Cotija cheese, crumbled

2 lime wedges, for garnish

To prepare the tortillas: In a large nonstick skillet over medium-high heat, add the olive oil. Once the oil is hot, add the tortillas and cook for 3 to 4 minutes, until the tortillas are sizzling and beginning to crisp. Flip the tortillas and sprinkle each with the Monterey Jack cheese. Lower the heat and let cook for an additional 1 to 3 minutes, until the cheese is mostly melted.

Top each tortilla with some of the shrimp, then add the slaw and radishes, and sprinkle with cotija cheese and the remaining cilantro garnish. Serve with lime wedges for squeezing juice over the tacos.

Blackened Halibut with Spring Pea Salad

Blackening is a Cajun cooking technique of dipping food in melted butter, then dredging it in spices and cooking it in a very hot cast-iron skillet. The brown-black color of the crust results from browned milk solids and charred spices. The duo of snap peas and English peas together with Meyer lemon and fresh mint lends a welcome brightness to this dish.

Cajun-Style Seasoning

2 teaspoons smoked paprika

2 teaspoons brown sugar

1 teaspoon smoked sea salt

½ teaspoon garlic powder

½ teaspoon onion powder

½ teaspoon dried oregano

¼ teaspoon black pepper

¼ teaspoon cayenne pepper

¼ teaspoon ground cumin

Spring Pea Salad

1½ tablespoons extra-virgin olive oil

1 tablespoon fresh Meyer lemon juice

2 teaspoons chopped mint leaves

1 teaspoon honey

1 teaspoon Dijon mustard

¼ teaspoon sea salt

¼ teaspoon freshly ground black pepper

1 cup snap peas, trimmed and strings removed

½ cup shelled English peas

¼ cup pea shoots, for garnish

Halibut

2 (6-ounce) halibut or cod fillets

1 tablespoon salted butter, melted

To make the Cajun seasoning: Whisk to combine the smoked paprika, brown sugar, sea salt, garlic powder, onion powder, oregano, black pepper, cayenne, and cumin. Set aside.

To make the spring pea salad: Whisk to combine the oil, lemon juice, mint, honey, mustard, salt, and pepper until well blended. Set aside.

Set a colander in the sink. In a saucepan, bring salted water to a boil. Add the snap peas to the boiling water for 2 minutes. Add the English peas and boil for an additional 1 to 2 minutes, until bright green, then drain them in a colander. In a bowl, add the snap peas, English peas, and the dressing, then toss lightly to coat. Set aside.

To cook the halibut: Heat a cast-iron skillet over high heat for 5 minutes. Turn the heat down to medium. Brush both sides of the halibut with melted butter, then sprinkle both sides generously with the Cajun seasoning. Carefully place the seasoned halibut in the hot skillet for 3 to 4 minutes, then gently turn over using a fish spatula or other large spatula and cook for another 2 to 3 minutes. The fish should be lightly browned on each side and firm and juicy when done, just becoming opaque inside.

Transfer the halibut to serving dishes along with spring pea salad. Garnish the salad with pea shoots.

Cook's Notes: The dry spices can be mixed ahead of time and stored at room temperature in an airtight container until ready to use.

In lieu of halibut, cod makes a perfectly fine substitute.

Seared Salmon with Mustard Glaze

This is an elegant and flavorful recipe that comes together very quickly. The ingredients in the glaze create a combination of sweet, savory, and spicy elements, with just enough vinegar and citrus to add a fresh brightness. The key to success is in the method of searing: starting with a very hot pan, timing each side, and checking the temperature so that the salmon is cooked perfectly tender.

Mustard Glaze

2½ tablespoons soy sauce

2 tablespoons maple syrup

1½ tablespoons whole grain (or stone-ground) mustard

2 tablespoons rice vinegar

2 teaspoons peeled and finely grated fresh ginger

1 garlic clove, minced

Pinch of red pepper flakes

Salmon

2 (6- to 8-ounce) salmon fillets (skin on), at room temperature

¼ teaspoon kosher salt

¼ teaspoon freshly ground black pepper

¼ cup all-purpose flour

1 tablespoon canola oil

1 tablespoon toasted sesame seeds

1 green onion, thinly sliced

2 lime wedges

To make the mustard glaze: In a small saucepan, combine the soy sauce, maple syrup, mustard, rice vinegar, ginger, garlic, and red pepper flakes. Simmer over a medium-low heat, stirring occasionally, for about 5 minutes, until thickened. Keep warm until ready to serve. (If making ahead, store in an airtight container in the refrigerator for up to 3 days.)

To prepare the salmon: Season the salmon fillets with the salt and pepper. Dredge both sides in the flour.

In a large nonstick skillet over medium heat, warm the canola oil. When the oil is hot, place the salmon fillets flesh side down in the skillet and cook for 3 minutes without moving. Using a fish spatula or other large spatula, carefully flip them over and continue to cook the skin side for 3 to 4 minutes, until the center is opaque and the internal temperature is 145°F.

Generously brush the glaze over the salmon and sprinkle with the toasted sesame seeds and green onion. Serve with the lime wedges to squeeze over the salmon before eating.

Prep Time: 30 minutes
Cook Time: 2 hours,
plus cooling time

Nanu's Chicken Enchiladas Verdes

This recipe comes from Cole's mom, who is a naturally wonderful cook. As a San Diego native who transplanted to Berkeley (she even worked on the garden at Chez Panisse in its early days), she knows how to whip up some Mexican food with a heavy California influence. This is an iteration of her beloved chicken enchiladas verdes, which is to say that together we documented her making a really good version of them, analyzing the best practices and methods that made sense for this book. But she won't ever make this version again—it's her nature to be always a little spontaneous and flexible in the kitchen. And she would encourage you to do the same!

2 large bone-in chicken breasts (about 1 pound)

3 tablespoons grapeseed oil

½ teaspoon kosher salt

¼ teaspoon freshly ground black pepper

1 small yellow onion, chopped

¼ teaspoon ground cumin

3 ounces Monterey Jack cheese, shredded

4 ounces Oaxacan cheese, shredded

2 ounces Cotija cheese, shredded

½ cup finely chopped cilantro, plus more for garnish (optional)

⅓ cup sliced green onions

1 (15-ounce) can green chile enchilada sauce

About ¼ cup canola or vegetable oil, for frying tortillas

Preheat the oven to 350°F. Line a rimmed baking sheet with parchment paper.

Place the chicken breasts, skin side up, on the baking sheet and drizzle with 2 tablespoons of the oil and sprinkle with salt and pepper. Roast for 45 minutes to 1 hour, until cooked through. Set aside to cool.

When the breasts are cool enough to handle, remove and discard the skin and bones and shred or pull the chicken apart into generous bite-size pieces.

In a skillet over medium-low heat, add the remaining 1 tablespoon of oil and sauté the onion, stirring until softened and translucent, 5 to 10 minutes. Add the cumin and cook while stirring until fully incorporated.

In a large bowl, add the shredded chicken, sautéed onion, Monterey Jack, 3 ounces of the Oaxacan cheese, Cotija cheese, cilantro, and green onions and toss until well combined. Set aside.

Spoon about 1 cup of the enchilada sauce into a 9 by 13-inch baking dish.

Create an assembly line for frying and filling the tortillas. In a large rimmed plate (or a 9- or 10-inch pie pan) set on a workspace near the stovetop, add about ½ cup of enchilada sauce, for dipping. In a large cast-iron griddle or skillet over medium-high heat, add 2 teaspoons of the canola oil. Dip a tortilla in the enchilada sauce to lightly coat, letting excess drip off. Carefully transfer the wet tortilla to the hot skillet and cook until puffed up and lightly browned on both sides, about 2 minutes on each side, using a large spatula to scrape (unstick) and flip the tortilla.

5 or 6 (10-inch) flour tortillas

⅓ cup grated Parmesan cheese

½ cup Mexican crema or sour cream

4 lime wedges

Cook's Notes: Frying the wet tortillas in a hot cast-iron skillet gets a little messy and will require a little elbow grease for scraping and turning, as the tortillas will want to stick to the pan. However, the complex flavor and texture it gives to this enchilada dish is worth it. You can alternatively use a nonstick skillet to make for a slightly smoother operation, but the texture of the tortillas will be slightly compromised.

Lay your fried tortilla down on a flat surface and spoon about ¾ cup of the filling across the center of the tortilla, leaving space around the edges. Fold the right and left sides in so they are partially covering the filling edges. While holding the folded sides in place, use your thumbs to start to lift the bottom of the tortilla up, and in a continuous motion, slide your hands in and fold the bottom half of the tortilla up and over the filling until it's a little more than covered. With both hands cupped around the tortilla-covered filling, pull the roll toward you as you "tuck" the bottom edge of the tortilla under and continue to tightly roll forward until secured. Follow this process for the remaining tortillas.

Place the enchiladas seam side down in the prepared baking dish, nestling next to each other. Pour the remaining sauce around the enchiladas (not on top). Lightly cover the tortillas with the remaining ounce of Oaxacan cheese and the Parmesan. Bake until the sauce is bubbling and the cheese is melted, 20 to 25 minutes. Let sit for 5 to 10 minutes before serving.

Serve with the Mexican crema and lime wedges and garnish with cilantro, if using.

To make ahead, cover the assembled baking dish with plastic wrap before the final bake and store in the refrigerator up to 1 day. Bring to room temperature before baking in a 350°F oven until heated through.

MAKES 4 SERVINGS

Prep Time: 45 minutes
Cook Time: 35 minutes

Chicken Katsu with Hawaiian Mac Salad

This dish is inspired by a Hawaiian takeout dinner that Cole introduced to me in our early years of dating in San Francisco. After our go-to restaurant closed, I tried my hand at re-creating it at home and was so pleased by the results that it's joined the rotation of weeknight dinners. When we make it for guests, we always advise them that even though the plating is intentionally segmented (a nod to the takeout style), the goal is to get a little of each item on the fork with every bite.

Salad

8 ounces dry elbow macaroni, cooked al dente, drained, and fully cooled

1 cup mayonnaise

1 tablespoon red wine vinegar

2 tablespoons minced celery

2 tablespoons chopped red onion

1 tablespoon finely grated yellow onion

1 small carrot, minced

1 red and/or orange bell pepper, seeded and chopped

2 teaspoons kosher salt

½ teaspoon freshly ground black pepper

Chicken

1 tablespoon grapeseed oil

2 cups panko bread crumbs

1¾ pounds boneless, skinless chicken thighs (5 or 6 pieces)

½ cup all-purpose flour

½ teaspoon kosher salt

½ teaspoon freshly ground black pepper

2 eggs, lightly beaten

3 cups cooked medium-grain white rice

¾ cup purchased katsu sauce

To make the salad: In a large bowl, add the macaroni, mayonnaise, vinegar, celery, both onions, carrot, bell pepper, salt, and black pepper. Mix well. Cover and store in the refrigerator until ready to use or up to 3 days in advance.

To make the chicken: In a large skillet over medium-high heat, add the grapeseed oil and heat until hot. Add the panko bread crumbs and cook, while stirring, until evenly toasted and a rich golden brown, 5 to 7 minutes. Set aside.

Preheat the oven to 400°F. Line a rimmed baking sheet with aluminum foil. Set a wire rack over the baking sheet and lightly grease it with grapeseed oil.

Place a chicken thigh between a folded piece of parchment paper and use the smooth side of a meat mallet (or rolling pin) to pound and flatten it to a thickness of about ¼ inch. Repeat with the remaining chicken.

In a bowl, whisk together the flour, salt, and black pepper. In a second bowl, add the beaten eggs. In a third bowl, add the toasted panko. Coat each piece of chicken first with flour, then dip it in the eggs, and finally coat with the panko.

Place the coated chicken on the wire rack set over the baking sheet and bake for about 25 minutes, flipping halfway through, until the chicken is crispy and no longer pink in the center and the internal temperature is 165°F.

To plate, place a rounded serving of rice into a small glass bowl. Use a spatula to pack it down into the bowl and flatten the top of the rice. Place the bowl upside down on a serving plate and lift the bowl away. Repeat with the macaroni salad. Use a sharp knife to cut the chicken crosswise into ½-inch strips and transfer it to the plate. Repeat for the other servings. Serve the katsu sauce on the side for dipping or drizzle it over the chicken.

Cornish Hen with Wild Rice Stuffing and Brown Butter Sage Sauce

A Cornish hen is well suited to be a hearty individual portion, or it can be halved to make a more modest meal. Roasting in a cast-iron skillet with a brown butter and sage sauce gives you crispy, caramelized skin and juicy and flavorful meat. The finished dish makes an impressive and elegant presentation but is still fairly simple to prepare. You can easily make this for a special date night in or when you have another couple joining you. This dish goes great with Roasted Beet Salad with Baby Arugula, Feta, and Edamame (page 76) and Poached Pears with Mulled Wine (page 188) for an elegant and festive dinner.

Stuffing

1 cup wild rice mix

2¼ cups chicken broth

2 tablespoons salted butter

1 shallot, finely chopped

¼ cup chopped dried apricots

½ cup chopped raw hazelnuts

1 tablespoon brown sugar

1 teaspoon fresh lemon juice

Pinch of freshly ground
black pepper

Sauce

4 tablespoons salted butter

5 or 6 sage leaves, chopped

¼ cup Frangelico

1 tablespoon brown sugar

2 teaspoons Dijon mustard

2 teaspoons rice vinegar

To make the stuffing: In a saucepan over medium-high heat, combine the rice, chicken broth, and 1 tablespoon of the butter and stir together. Bring to a boil, stirring once before lowering the heat to a simmer. Cover and cook until the liquid is absorbed, about 30 minutes.

While the rice is cooking, melt the remaining 1 tablespoon of butter in a sauté pan over medium-low heat. Add the shallot and cook for about 2 minutes, until softened. Add the apricots, hazelnuts, brown sugar, lemon juice, and pepper. Cook while stirring for another minute, or until evenly combined. Turn off the heat. Add the cooked rice, stirring to combine. Set the stuffing aside.

To make the sauce: In a sauté pan or skillet over medium-high heat, melt the butter. Continue to cook, stirring frequently, until the butter has foamed and chestnut-brown flecks begin to appear, along with a nutty aroma. Turn the heat down to low, add the sage, and cook while stirring for 1 to 2 minutes, until the sage leaves are fragrant and slightly crisp. Add the Frangelico, brown sugar, mustard, and vinegar and let simmer for about 5 minutes, stirring occasionally, until well blended and reduced slightly. Set aside.

To make the Cornish hens: Preheat the oven to 400°F. Remove the giblets from the cavity of the Cornish hens. Rinse the hens thoroughly, inside and out, and pat dry with the paper towels.

CONTINUED

CONTINUED

Cornish Hen with Wild Rice Stuffing and Brown Butter Sage Sauce

Cornish Hens

2 (1½-pound) Cornish hens

1 teaspoon kosher salt

¼ teaspoon freshly ground black pepper

Rub both the inside and outside of the Cornish hens with a mixture of the salt and pepper. Gently stuff each hen's cavity with about 1 cup of the stuffing until loosely filled. Tuck the wings under the hen and tie the ends of the legs together with twine.

Place the hens breast side up in a cast-iron skillet, and roast in the oven for 10 minutes before lowering the oven temperature to 350°F. Continue to roast for about 40 minutes, brushing the hens liberally with the sauce every 10 to 15 minutes, until the internal temperature of the thickest part of the breast and the stuffing measures 165°F. If you want crispier, browned skins, broil on low in the oven for about 3 minutes, until the skins are slightly darker, but not burned.

Using a sharp knife, split the hens lengthwise down the center of the breastbone or serve whole, spooning the pan juices over them. Serve with any remaining wild rice stuffing.

Prep Time: 50 minutes,
plus cooling time
Cook Time: 4 to 5 hours

Braised Short Ribs with Porcini Mushrooms over Creamy Mashed Potatoes

This is a dish that will make you want to pick the bones and savor every last morsel of beef rib deliciousness, then pick up the plate and lick every drop of the luxurious sauce. When perfectly braised beef ribs meet nutty, earthy porcini mushrooms, it's a match made in heaven. To achieve complete harmony, serve on a cloud of the creamiest-ever mashed potatoes.

Short Ribs

¼ cup dry porcini mushrooms

½ cup hot water

4 beef bone-in short ribs (about 2 pounds)

¼ teaspoon kosher salt

¼ teaspoon freshly ground black pepper

1 tablespoon olive oil

2 ounces chopped pancetta

½ cup diced onions

½ cup diced carrots

½ cup diced celery

2 tablespoons all-purpose flour

2 garlic cloves, minced

2 tablespoons tomato paste

1 cup dry red wine (Cabernet Sauvignon works nicely)

1 teaspoon Dijon mustard

1 bay leaf

1 teaspoon chopped rosemary

1 teaspoon chopped thyme

4 cups beef stock

To make the ribs: Rehydrate the porcini mushrooms by submerging them in the hot water for 10 minutes.

Preheat the oven to 300°F. Dry the ribs thoroughly with paper towels, then season them with the salt and pepper.

In a large Dutch oven over medium-high heat, add the oil and heat until shimmering. Working in batches, so as to not crowd the pan, sear the short ribs on all sides until golden brown. Set aside.

Add the pancetta to the pan and cook over medium heat until it starts to brown, about 4 minutes. Stir in the onions, carrots, and celery and cook until softened, about 5 minutes. Sprinkle in the flour and cook, stirring well, until the flour begins to brown. Stir in the garlic and tomato paste and cook until incorporated, 1 to 2 minutes.

Pour in the wine and bring to a boil, stirring. Let simmer until the wine is reduced by half. Stir in the mustard, bay leaf, rosemary, and thyme.

Return the ribs to the pan. Add about 3 cups of the beef stock or enough to just cover the ribs. Cover the pan and place it in the oven for 3 hours, or until the meat is tender, stirring the sauce and turning the ribs halfway through cooking.

Using tongs, remove the ribs from the pot and set them aside to cool. Discard the bay leaf and any bones that may have separated from the meat.

Let the stew cool slightly. Use an immersion blender or blender to puree the vegetables in the liquid until smooth. Pour the sauce through a strainer to remove and discard any remaining solids. Return the strained sauce to the pan and thicken the sauce, if needed, by continuing to simmer it over medium-low heat, or add additional beef stock or water if it is too thick. Return the ribs to the sauce to gently reheat them before serving.

CONTINUED

Braised Short Ribs with Porcini Mushrooms over Creamy Mashed Potatoes

Mashed Potatoes

4 large russet potatoes (about 3½ pounds)

2 teaspoons extra-virgin olive oil

1 teaspoon kosher salt

¼ teaspoon freshly ground black pepper

½ cup warm milk

2 ounces cream cheese, at room temperature

3 tablespoons salted butter, at room temperature

2 tablespoons sour cream, at room temperature

Cook's Notes: The braised short ribs are ideal for preparing a day in advance as the texture of the meat and the flavors further improve with the extra time, and you can easily remove and discard solidified fat from the surface.

To make the mashed potatoes: Preheat the oven to 425°F. Line a baking sheet with aluminum foil. Drizzle the potatoes with the oil and rub it into skins. Sprinkle with ½ teaspoon of the kosher salt. Pierce the top of each potato twice with a fork. Bake for 45 minutes to 1 hour, until fork-tender.

When just cool enough to handle, cut the potatoes in half lengthwise and use a spoon to scoop out the white part into a large bowl, discarding the skins. Use a masher (or press it through a ricer) to eliminate lumps.

Add the remaining ½ teaspoon of salt, the pepper, and ¼ cup of the warm milk and stir with a wooden spoon until incorporated. Stir in the remaining ¼ cup milk. Finally, stir in the sour cream, 2 tablespoons of the butter, and the cream cheese until well combined. Using a whisk or hand mixer at medium-low speed, whip the potatoes for 1 to 2 minutes, until just smooth, light, and creamy.

Grease a baking dish with the remaining 1 tablespoon of butter. Transfer the potatoes to the baking dish and return them to the oven for 10 to 15 minutes, until hot. Serve warm. (If making ahead, cover the assembled baking dish with plastic wrap before the final bake and store it in the refrigerator for up to 2 days. To reheat, bring to room temperature, then bake in a 425°F oven, covered with foil, for about 20 minutes, or until hot.)

Serve the ribs with sauce over the creamy mashed potatoes.

Pan-Grilled Pork Chops and Pineapples with Pineapple Rum Glaze

Oh, perfectly pan-grilled pork chops with pineapple rum glaze, where have you been all my life? Why have I suffered through so many thin, dry, tough chops? I solemnly swear I will seek out thick-cut pork chops from the butcher counter from now on. I will always use a grill pan and oven to finish my chops, testing the temperature and following the directions below.

I hope it's not too late to change the way you feel about pork chops as well, as they are a nice, easy weeknight meal to work into your rotation.

Glaze

½ cup diced fresh pineapple

3 tablespoons brown sugar

2 tablespoons salted butter

2 tablespoons rum

1 teaspoon apple cider vinegar

¼ teaspoon salt

Pork Chops

2 (1½-inch-thick) pork chops, about 2 pounds, preferably bone-in

2 tablespoons canola oil

2 teaspoons kosher salt

¼ teaspoon freshly ground black pepper

Pineapples

3 thick round slices of fresh pineapple, peeled

2 tablespoons salted butter, melted

1 tablespoon brown sugar

To make the glaze: In a small saucepan over medium-high heat, place the pineapple, brown sugar, butter, rum, vinegar, and salt and simmer, stirring occasionally, until the mixture has thickened, 8 to 10 minutes. Keep warm until ready to serve. (If making ahead, store in an airtight container in the refrigerator for up to 3 days.)

To make the pork chops: Preheat the oven to 400°F. Take the pork chops out of the refrigerator about 20 minutes before cooking. Rub both sides with the oil and season generously with the salt and pepper.

Preheat an ovenproof grill pan (or skillet) over high heat until very hot. Place the pork chops on the grill pan and cook for 2 minutes without moving, then flip and cook for another 2 minutes, or until seared with grill marks on both sides. Transfer the pork chops in the grill pan to the oven and roast for 6 minutes. Remove from the oven, spoon or brush the glaze over the top of the pork chops, then return to the oven for 5 to 8 minutes, or until the internal temperature reaches 145°F. Transfer the pork chops to a plate and allow to rest before serving.

To make the pineapples: While the pork chops are resting, heat a grill pan over medium-high heat until hot. Using a pastry brush, coat both sides of the pineapple slices with the butter and sprinkle with the brown sugar. Place the pineapple slices on the grill pan and cook for about 3 minutes on each side, until charred with grill marks on both sides.

Serve the pork chops drizzled with the glaze and alongside the grilled pineapples.

Cook's Note: Insert an instant-read thermometer into the thickest part of the chop without touching any bone. The pork chops should be cooked to an internal temperature of 145°F.

Udon Stir-Fry with Pork and Baby Bok Choy

Udon noodles, most often found in Japanese soups, also work wonderfully in a stir-fried noodle dish. The baby bok choy is a wonderfully easy vegetable to prepare and adds some green to your dish, and a hint of lime brightens the flavorful broth.

2 tablespoons mirin

2 tablespoons soy sauce

2 teaspoons gochujang (or a chili paste like sambal oelek)

2 teaspoons fresh lime juice

1 tablespoon brown sugar

6 ounces boneless pork loin chop, cut across the grain into ¼-inch-thick strips

2 teaspoons cornstarch

8 ounces fresh, frozen, or dried udon noodles

1 tablespoon canola oil

8 to 10 ounces baby bok choy, halved (or quartered if large)

Pinch of kosher salt

2 green onions, pale green parts only, cut on the diagonal into ¾-inch pieces, reserving the dark green tops for garnish (optional)

1 small garlic clove, minced

2 lime wedges, for garnish

In a bowl, whisk to combine the mirin, soy sauce, gochujang, lime juice, and brown sugar. Reserve 2 tablespoons in a small bowl and set aside.

Add the pork strips to the bowl of marinade, sprinkle the cornstarch on top, and toss to coat. Let sit for about 10 minutes.

Bring a large pot of salted water to a boil. Add the udon noodles, stir, and cook according to package directions until tender but not overly soft. Drain the noodles, reserving a ladleful of the cooking water. Rinse the noodles with very cold water until cool. Set aside.

Heat a large skillet or wok over high heat until hot. Swirl in 2 teaspoons of the canola oil and heat until shimmering. Place the pork strips in the skillet in a single layer, discarding the starchy marinade. Cook the pork undisturbed for 1 minute or until browned. Toss and continue to cook for another 1 to 2 minutes, until evenly browned and almost cooked through. Transfer to a bowl and set aside. Wipe the skillet with a paper towel.

In the skillet over medium-high heat, heat the remaining 1 teaspoon canola oil until hot. Add the baby bok choy, cut sides down, and season with the salt. Cook, turning occasionally, until tender, about 5 minutes. (Cover the skillet with a lid for 1 minute or so to help soften the stems). Add the green onions and garlic and cook while stirring until fragrant, 1 to 2 minutes.

Add the cooked noodles, the pork, and the reserved 2 tablespoons of marinade to the skillet, toss with the bok choy mixture until combined, then turn off the heat. If the noodles seem too sticky, mix in some of the reserved noodle water, 1 tablespoon at time. Transfer to a serving dish and garnish with a lime wedge and dark green tops of green onions, if using.

Cook's Notes: To incorporate the bok choy in smaller bites, cut it crosswise into smaller pieces, but add the stem sections to the pan sooner than the leaves, as they do take longer to cook.

The pork loin will be easier to cut into strips when very cold.

Prep Time: 20 minutes
Cook Time: 1 hour

Country Meat Loaf

Meat loaf has a bad name. Just think about it—loaf of meat? Okay, now that we've deconstructed the word, let's start over. This meat loaf is packed with flavor, from its foundation of caramelized onion, carrot, and thyme to the special glaze that gets both mixed into the mixture and spread over all but the underside of the meat loaf. If there are any leftovers, I highly recommend melting some butter in a skillet and browning both sides. They are also great on a sandwich!

Glaze

¼ cup ketchup

1 tablespoon Worcestershire sauce

1 teaspoon oyster sauce

½ teaspoon brown sugar

¼ teaspoon garlic powder

¼ teaspoon dry mustard

¼ teaspoon prepared horseradish

¼ teaspoon hot sauce

Meat Loaf

1 tablespoon olive oil

1 small yellow onion, minced

1 carrot, minced

1 small garlic clove, minced

¼ teaspoon chopped thyme

¼ cup beef broth

1 teaspoon apple cider vinegar

1 cup fresh bread crumbs

8 ounces ground beef

3 ounces sweet Italian sausages, casings removed and broken apart into pieces

1 egg

1 tablespoon finely chopped flat-leaf parsley

To make the glaze: In a small bowl, whisk together the ketchup, Worcestershire, oyster sauce, brown sugar, garlic powder, dry mustard, horseradish, and hot sauce. Set aside.

To make the meat loaf: Preheat the oven to 375°F. Line a rimmed baking sheet with parchment paper.

In a sauté pan over medium-low heat, warm the oil. Add the onion, carrot, garlic, and thyme and sauté, stirring occasionally, until the onion and carrot have softened and are just starting to brown, 10 to 15 minutes.

Add the broth and vinegar, scraping the bottom of the pan with a spatula to mix in any brown bits, and cook until the liquid has mostly evaporated, about 5 minutes. Set aside and let cool slightly.

In a bowl, mix the sautéed onion and carrot mixture, the bread crumbs, and half of the glaze until well combined. Add the beef, sausages, egg, and parsley and gently toss until just combined.

Transfer the meat loaf onto the prepared baking sheet and shape into a compact rectangular loaf shape about 4 by 6 inches. Brush the top and all sides of the meat loaf using the remaining glaze.

Bake for about 30 minutes, until the meat is cooked through and has an internal temperature of 160°F. Let rest for a few minutes before serving. If making ahead, let it cool before wrapping it in foil and storing it in an airtight container in the refrigerator for up to 3 days. Place the foil-wrapped loaf on a baking sheet and reheat until warm.

Prep Time: 15 minutes, plus
20 minutes chilling time
Cook Time: 30 minutes

Indoor Filet Mignon Steaks with Bacon and Blue Cheese Compound Butter

The secret to cooking the perfect pan-seared filet mignon is to combine pan searing with an oven finish. This gives you a slightly crusted exterior with a juicy, tender interior. A few basic rules for cooking steak this way: Get the pan hot, keep your steaks dry, and make sure the cooking area is well ventilated. This super-tender cut of beef does need a little support in the flavor and fat department. That's where both the bacon and blue-cheese compound butter come in—the ultimate wingmen.

Compound Butter

4 tablespoons unsalted butter, at room temperature

1 ounce crumbled blue cheese

¼ teaspoon smoked sea salt

¼ teaspoon coarse ground black pepper

Steaks

2 slices bacon

2 (6- to 8-ounce) filet mignon steaks, 1½ to 2 inches thick, at room temperature

½ teaspoon coarse kosher salt

½ teaspoon coarsely ground black pepper

1 tablespoon avocado oil

To make the compound butter: In a small bowl, add the butter, blue cheese, sea salt, and pepper and mix until evenly distributed. Place the butter mixture in the center of piece of plastic wrap or wax paper. Roll the bottom half of the wrap over the butter, form it into a compact log, and roll until fully wrapped. Twist the sides to seal and refrigerate for at least 20 minutes or up to 5 days in advance.

To make the steaks: Preheat the oven to 400°F.

Wrap the bacon around the sides of the steaks and secure it with toothpicks.

Pat the steaks dry. Season the top and bottom of steaks generously with the salt and pepper, pressing it into the filets.

Heat a cast-iron skillet over medium-high heat until very hot and just starting to smoke, about 2 minutes. Add the oil to the skillet and swirl the pan until evenly coated. Add the steaks to the skillet and sear them without moving for 4 minutes, until a well-browned crust has formed around the bottom edge. Using tongs, flip the steaks over and cook for 3 to 4 minutes before transferring the skillet with the steaks to the oven. Cook until the desired level of doneness is achieved. For medium rare, cook in the oven for about 6 minutes, flipping the steaks halfway through. Check the internal temperature toward the center of the steak with an instant-read thermometer. (It should read 130°F for medium rare.)

Transfer the steaks to a serving dish and cover loosely with aluminum foil. Let rest for 5 to 10 minutes. Serve with a generous pat of the compound butter on top of each steak.

Cook's Note: Check for the desired doneness with a meat thermometer (preferably an instant-read one). Most steak lovers prefer the internal temperature of 130°F to 135°F (after resting), or medium rare, for the juiciest, most tender filets.

Chili Quinoa Bowls

This casual hearty meal is good for a crowd if you scale up the ingredients. Serve assembled in bowls or with toppings separately so you can individualize to your liking. The chili can be made up to 2 days ahead and refrigerated, and most of the toppings can be prepared a day ahead, with the exception of the avocado, cilantro, and crispy tortilla strips.

1 tablespoon olive oil

1 small yellow onion, chopped

1 pound ground turkey

1 garlic clove, minced

2 tablespoons chili powder

1 tablespoon kosher salt

¼ teaspoon cayenne powder

1 (14½-ounce) can crushed tomatoes

1 (15-ounce) can black beans, drained and rinsed

1 cup water, plus more if needed

1 tablespoon agave nectar

1 tablespoon Worcestershire sauce

3 cups cooked quinoa

4 lime wedges, for garnish

12 store-bought tortilla chips or crispy Tortilla Strips (page 64)

¼ cup shredded Cheddar cheese

¼ cup Mexican crema (or sour cream)

1 cup grape or cherry tomatoes, halved

2 ripe avocados, cut into ⅓-inch slices

¼ cup chopped cilantro

In a Dutch oven or heavy skillet over medium heat, warm the oil. Add the onion and sauté until soft and translucent, about 5 minutes. Increase the heat to medium-high and add the turkey, garlic, chili powder, salt, and cayenne. Cook, using a wooden spoon to combine the ingredients and break apart the meat, for 5 to 7 minutes, until the meat is no longer pink.

Add the tomatoes, beans, water, agave nectar, and Worcestershire, stirring to combine, and bring to a boil. Turn the heat down to low and let simmer uncovered for about 30 minutes, stirring occasionally, until the chili has thickened and some of the liquid has cooked off. If making ahead, let the chili cool slightly before storing it in an airtight container in the refrigerator for up to 3 days or in the freezer for up to 2 months. Let it thaw overnight in the refrigerator before reheating until warm.

Divide the cooked quinoa among 4 bowls and top with the chili. Garnish with lime wedges and offer the tortilla strips, Cheddar cheese, crema, tomatoes, avocado, and cilantro on the side.

Prep Time: 10 minutes
Cook Time: 10 minutes

The Greatest Lamb Burgers in the World (Almost)

The passion for cooking (and eating) in both of our families runs strong. My brother-in-law once spent half a day searching the county for the perfect bun for his lamb burgers—and nobody stopped him because his lamb burgers are indeed perfection. We eagerly wait to enjoy the fruits of an all-day lamb-burger grocery-store forage. This, here, is not the greatest lamb burger in the world. No. This is just a tribute.

Yogurt Sauce

½ English cucumber, peeled, seeded, and thinly sliced

1 teaspoon kosher salt

¾ cup Greek yogurt

1 tablespoon chopped mint

1 tablespoon chopped cilantro

2 teaspoons chopped dill

2 teaspoons lemon zest

2 small garlic cloves, minced

Pinch of freshly ground black pepper

Lamb Burgers

1 pound ground lamb

¼ cup finely chopped mint

2 tablespoons extra-virgin olive oil

1 teaspoon ground cumin

1 teaspoon kosher salt, plus more as needed

¼ teaspoon freshly ground black pepper, plus more as needed

2 kaiser rolls, halved crosswise and lightly toasted

1½ ounces goat cheese, whipped until spreadable

½ cup arugula microgreens or baby arugula

To make the yogurt sauce: Place the cucumber slices, sprinkled with the salt, on paper towels. Let sit for 15 minutes to get rid of excess moisture. Set aside.

In a bowl, whisk together the yogurt, mint, cilantro, dill, lemon zest, garlic, and pepper. Add the cucumber and stir to combine. Cover and store in the refrigerator until ready to use.

To make the lamb burgers: In a large bowl, add the lamb, mint, oil, cumin, salt, and pepper, and gently toss with your hands until just evenly combined. Divide the meat into two portions and gently shape them into patties about 4 inches wide and 1 inch thick each. Use your fingers to make a wide, shallow indentation on the top center of each patty.

Heat a cast-iron skillet over medium-high heat. Season the patties on both sides with additional salt and pepper. Add the patties to the skillet and cook them, undisturbed, until lightly charred on the bottom, 3 to 4 minutes. Flip the patties over and cook for an additional 2 to 3 minutes for medium-rare doneness with an internal temperature of 125°F. Remove the patties from the skillet to a plate and allow them to rest for 2 to 3 minutes.

To assemble the burgers, spread the cucumber-yogurt sauce on the inside top of each bun. Place the burger on the bottom half of the bun, add the goat cheese and arugula, and cover with the top half of the bun.

Desserts

Prep Time: 5½ hours
(includes inactive time)
Cook Time: 5 minutes,
plus cooling time

Ginger Beer, Lime, and Mint Granita with Candied Mint Leaves

The ginger flavor in this granita marries well with lime and mint and makes a refreshing icy dessert on a hot day. It's also a perfect dessert after you might have overindulged on something delicious, such as, say, Nanu's Chicken Enchiladas Verdes (page 164), as ginger soothes an upset stomach. This is very easy to put together and is also forgiving on the timing of stirring with a fork to help the crystals form. Skipping a stirring or going a longer period of time between stirrings will still yield a great result.

2 cups ginger beer

3 tablespoons fresh lime juice

1 teaspoon lime zest

6 large mint leaves, coarsely chopped

12 whole mint leaves

4 teaspoons honey

1 pasteurized egg white, beaten until foamy

¼ cup granulated sugar

In a saucepan over low heat, add the ginger beer, lime juice, lime zest, chopped mint, and honey. Bring to a simmer, stirring to combine. Remove from the heat and let cool completely.

Pour the cooled liquid through a strainer into a rectangular freezer-safe dish, discarding the remaining solids. Place in the freezer for 45 minutes to 1 hour, or until the mixture starts to solidify. Stir the mixture thoroughly with a fork to break it up. Return to the freezer and repeat scraping and stirring with a fork every 30 minutes for about 4 hours, or until it is crystallized and frozen. Serve within 1 to 2 days.

To make the candied mint leaves, working with one whole mint leaf at a time, brush one side of the leaf with the beaten egg white. Holding the leaf over a small bowl, sprinkle with sugar. Turn the leaf over and repeat on other side. Repeat for the remaining whole leaves. Place on a wire rack or a piece of parchment paper to dry completely. (If making ahead, store them in an airtight container at room temperature for up 2 days.)

To serve the granita, scrape with a fork to loosen, then scoop into chilled serving bowls or glasses. Garnish with the candied mint leaves.

Poached Pears with Mulled Wine

These poached pears are an elegant, impressive dessert that requires no baking and can be made ahead of time. They also pair (pear!) very well with Vanilla Bean Whipped Cream (page 33) or Mom's Best Ever Coffee Ice Cream (page 195) and a sprinkle of chopped candied pecans.

But wait! There's more! You'll get mulled wine that you can pour into a thermos and take outside into the crisp fall air to enjoy a fall sunset while it's still happening at a reasonable hour to have a drink.

Candied Pecans

1 tablespoon brown sugar

1 teaspoon salted butter

½ teaspoon water

Pinch of ground cardamom

Pinch of kosher salt

¼ cup raw pecan halves

Pears

1 bottle (750 ml) dry red wine (Cabernet Sauvignon or Merlot)

½ cup granulated sugar

¼ cup honey

2 tablespoons tawny port

1 teaspoon vanilla bean paste or vanilla extract

Zest and juice of ½ orange

1 blood orange, cut into ¼-inch-thick slices, reserving 2 for garnish

4 cloves

2 star anise

2 cinnamon sticks

2 firm Bosc pears, peeled, with stems left intact

To make the candied pecans: In a skillet over medium heat, combine the brown sugar, butter, water, cardamom, and salt and cook, stirring until well combined and bubbling. Add the pecans, stir to coat, and cook for another 2 to 3 minutes, until the brown sugar mixture is thick and syrupy. Using a spatula, carefully spread the pecans out in a single layer onto a parchment-lined baking sheet and let cool completely. Break apart when hardened and dry to the touch, 2 to 3 hours. Store in an airtight container at room temperature for up to 2 weeks.

To make the pears: In a saucepan over low heat, add the wine, granulated sugar, honey, port, vanilla bean paste, orange zest and juice, blood orange slices, cloves, star anise, and cinnamon sticks. Cook while gently stirring until the sugar is dissolved. Increase the heat to medium-high and let boil for 3 to 5 minutes.

Turn the heat down to low, add the pears, cover and let simmer, spooning the liquid over pears occasionally, for about 30 minutes, or until pears are just tender when pierced with a knife. Remove from the heat and let the pears cool to room temperature in the liquid.

Store the pears in an airtight container, submerged in the mulled wine, and refrigerate for at least 4 hours and up to 2 days.

Reheat the pears in the mulled wine in a saucepan over low heat until warm. Serve the pears whole or sliced in half lengthwise and spoon some of the mulled wine on top. Garnish with the pecans and a blood orange slice.

Cook's Notes: If you wish to plate these pears standing upright for a more elegant presentation, cut a sliver off the bottom of the pears before poaching them to create a flat surface.

Refrigerating the pears in their liquid after poaching allows the pears to turn a deeper red color, but it can be skipped if necessary.

Prep Time: 20 minutes,
plus chilling time
Cook Time: 40 minutes,
plus cooling time

Strawberry-Rhubarb Biscuits

You will become a biscuit aficionado if you follow these few simple steps to creating the tallest, most tender, flaky biscuits. Start with very cold butter and cream, and handle the dough gently and as little as possible—the dough needs enough moisture to feel somewhat sticky. When shaping the dough, pat it gently to the desired shape and thickness, adding flour to your hands rather than to the dough as needed. When cutting, use a sharp knife or cookie cutter dipped in flour and cut straight down in one motion; do not twist or saw, as this will seal the edges and keep them from rising to their full height. If the dough becomes warm, pop it in the refrigerator for 15 to 20 minutes before baking. Start with a hot oven and watch them closely.

Biscuits

1⅓ cups (160 grams) all-purpose flour, plus more for dusting

1 tablespoon baking powder

2 teaspoons granulated sugar

¼ teaspoon kosher salt

4 tablespoons cold unsalted butter, cut into small cubes

½ cup plus 2 tablespoons cold heavy cream, plus more as needed

Raw cane sugar, preferably demerara, for sprinkling tops before baking

To make the biscuits: Preheat the oven to 425°F. Line a baking sheet with parchment paper.

In a large mixing bowl, whisk the flour, baking powder, granulated sugar, and salt to combine.

Toss the butter into the flour mixture and cut it in with a pastry blender or 2 knives until the butter is just coated in flour and is in pea-size pieces. Make a well in the flour mixture. Pour the cream into the flour well and mix with a fork until just incorporated. If the mixture appears dry, add additional cream in tablespoon increments until the dough looks wet.

Turn the dough onto a lightly floured wood board and using flour-coated hands, gently gather and pat the dough into a 4¼-inch square that is approximately 1½ to 2 inches thick. Use a sharp knife dipped into flour to cut straight down around the outside border, trimming to make straight, clean edges and discarding the trimmed dough. Cut the biscuits into 4 squares, about 2 by 2 inches.

Arrange the biscuits on the prepared baking sheet so that the sides of biscuits are about 2 inches apart. Brush the biscuit tops with heavy cream and sprinkle with the raw cane sugar. Bake for about 15 minutes, rotating the baking sheet halfway through, until golden brown on top. Set aside to cool on a wire rack.

Compote

12 ounces rhubarb (about 4 stalks), ends trimmed, cut into 1-inch pieces

¾ cup firmly packed brown sugar

2 tablespoons salted butter, melted

1 tablespoon fresh orange juice (or ½ teaspoon fresh lemon juice)

1 teaspoon vanilla bean paste or vanilla extract

1 cup quartered strawberries

Whipped Cream

¾ cup cold heavy cream

2 teaspoons sifted confectioners' sugar

To make the compote: Preheat the oven to 375°F. On a rimmed baking sheet, add the rhubarb, brown sugar, butter, orange juice, and vanilla bean paste and toss to combine. Roast the rhubarb, stirring occasionally, for about 15 minutes, until the rhubarb is tender but still bright and intact. Strain the liquid from the rhubarb into a saucepan and set the rhubarb pieces aside. Cook the rhubarb juices over a medium-low heat until slightly reduced with a syrup-like consistency. Add the roasted rhubarb and the fresh strawberries into the saucepan and toss to coat. Allow to cool slightly before serving.

To make the whipped cream: Place the mixing bowl and whisk in the freezer for at least 15 minutes to chill. In a stand mixer fitted with the whisk attachment, beat the cream on medium-high for 1 minute. Decrease the speed to low, add the confectioners' sugar, and return to medium-high. Mix for another 30 seconds, or until cream just starts to form soft to medium peaks. Cover and refrigerate for up to 2 hours before serving.

Once the biscuits have cooled, split them in half crosswise. On the bottom half of each biscuit, spoon on some of the roasted rhubarb and strawberries and top with a dollop of the whipped cream. Replace the top of the biscuit and serve immediately.

To make the biscuits ahead, freeze the cut dough rounds first on a baking sheet and then transfer them to an airtight container. Bake them directly from the freezer at 400°F for 20 minutes.

Cook's Note: Poached Pears with Mulled Wine (page 188) are a great alternative in the fall when rhubarb and strawberries are not in season.

Prep Time: 15 minutes,
plus 2 hours chilling time
Cook Time: 40 minutes,
plus 10 minutes cooling time

Blackberry Crumble

This dessert is so simple to make, but it has the allure of a freshly baked, more labor-intensive blackberry pie. Pro tip: Topping the warm crumble with a few scoops of a good vanilla bean ice cream while still in the pie pan makes this dessert a home run. Sadly, if you go that route, it will have to be eaten in its entirety right away because, oops, the ice cream won't keep. So grab a couple of spoons and get to work like the pros you are.

Crumble Topping

½ cup all-purpose flour

1 tablespoon cornstarch

¼ cup firmly packed brown sugar

6 gingersnap cookies, finely chopped

4 tablespoons unsalted butter, melted

Fruit Filling

1 pint blackberries

¼ cup granulated sugar

½ tablespoon fresh lemon juice

1 tablespoon unsalted butter, for coating the pie pan

Vanilla bean ice cream (optional)

Whipped Cream (page 191; optional)

Cook's Note: Use firm, crispy gingersnap cookies to achieve a crumble topping with just the right amount of crunch.

To make the crumble topping: Whisk together the flour, cornstarch, brown sugar, and gingersnaps in a bowl. Pour in the melted butter and stir until fully incorporated and no dry flour remains. Cover the bowl with plastic wrap and chill in the refrigerator for at least 2 hours, until you can break the mixture apart into sturdy, medium-size crumbles.

To make the fruit filling: Gently toss together blackberries, granulated sugar, and lemon juice in a bowl. Set aside.

Preheat the oven to 350°F. Grease an 8-inch pie pan with the unsalted butter.

Put the fruit in the pie pan and top with the crumbles. Bake for 30 to 40 minutes, until the fruit center is bubbling hot and the crumble topping is lightly browned. Let sit at room temperature for 5 to 10 minutes before serving.

Serve warm with vanilla bean ice cream or whipped cream, if desired.

Prep Time: 30 minutes,
plus 10 hours chilling time
Cook Time: 10 minutes

Mom's Best Ever Coffee Ice Cream

My mom is as fantastic at making desserts as she is at cooking, but you'll never catch her bragging. Ironically, she would never call anything of hers "the best ever," but whenever she is learning how to make a new dish, she begins by typing "best ever [name of whatever dish]" into a search engine. She has fine-tuned this coffee ice cream recipe over the years all on her own. I am proud to proclaim (even if she won't) that it is actually "the best ever," and I'm even more proud that we can share it with you.

2 cups heavy cream

1 cup whole milk

1 cup granulated sugar

2½ teaspoons espresso powder

Pinch of kosher salt

1 tablespoon Kahlúa

1 teaspoon vanilla extract

Whipped Cream
(page 191; optional)

Dark chocolate shavings
(optional; see Cook's Note)

In a saucepan over medium heat, add the cream, milk, sugar, espresso powder, and salt. Heat until just beginning to simmer, stirring until the sugar and espresso powder have completely dissolved. Turn off the heat and stir in the Kahlúa and vanilla. Transfer to an airtight container and refrigerate overnight or for at least 6 hours.

Add the chilled mixture to your ice cream maker and churn according to the manufacturer's instructions or to soft-serve consistency, about 20 minutes.

Quickly transfer the mixture to an airtight container or loaf pan and cover the surface with plastic wrap (and replace the lid of the container, if using). Freeze for at least 4 hours or until firm. Store in the freezer for up to 3 weeks.

Serve with a dollop of whipped cream and sprinkle with chocolate shavings, if desired.

Cook's Notes: To make the chocolate shavings, use a y-peeler or paring knife to slice flat, thin shavings from a room-temperature piece of dark chocolate.

An ice cream maker is a space hog, but it's also generally a reasonably-priced specialty appliance. If fresh homemade ice cream made with simple ingredients sounds exciting, you might want to make room for one.

Sweet Kiera's Chocolate Chip Cookies

If this book was a living, breathing thing, this chocolate chip cookie would be its heart. It's my heart. Trying to bake the best chocolate chip cookie ever for my new beau, I started to dig deep into the science of baking. This cookie (or all the versions of this cookie that got me here) is what made me fall in love with baking while I was falling in love with Cole. We often send a batch to our wedding clients to say "thank you," and it has become expected that I will bring them to social gatherings. I was even packing cookies (still warm from the oven) into my hospital bag the night I went into labor so that we could give them to our unborn daughter's nurses. (They almost wouldn't let us check out of the hospital without providing the recipe.) Once upon a time, I thought I would die with this recipe clenched in my hands. Now I couldn't be more excited to share it with you.

Brown Butter

1 cup (8 ounces)
unsalted butter

Cookies

1 cup granulated sugar

1 tablespoon molasses

1 teaspoon vanilla bean
paste or vanilla extract

1 egg plus 1 egg yolk

2 cups (240 grams)
all-purpose flour

1 teaspoon kosher salt

1 teaspoon baking powder

½ teaspoon baking soda

½ teaspoon espresso powder
(optional)

6 ounces bittersweet
chocolate (60 to 70 percent),
coarsely chopped

1 teaspoon flaky sea salt, for
sprinkling on the dough

To make the brown butter: In a stainless steel sauté pan set over low heat, melt the butter, stirring occasionally to encourage even melting. Once fully melted, increase the heat to medium and continue to cook, stirring occasionally, until the mixture starts to sizzle and bubble, about 3 minutes. Continue to cook, stirring frequently and running a rubber spatula around the bottom and sides of the pan, until the butter starts to foam, 1 to 2 minutes. Once there is a full layer of foam on top, brown specks will start to appear on the bottom of the pan at a rapid pace. (You can turn the heat down a little at this point if the browning is happening too fast.) Continue to cook, stirring constantly, until many brown flecks are visible and the butter turns a rich amber brown, 1 to 3 minutes. Carefully transfer to a heatproof bowl and let cool slightly. Cover and store in the refrigerator until cool and solidified, about 2 hours, or in the freezer for about 30 minutes.

To make the cookies: In a stand mixer fitted with the paddle attachment, cream the chilled brown butter and sugar together until light and fluffy, 3 to 5 minutes. Add the molasses, vanilla bean paste, and egg and egg yolk, and mix on low until just combined.

Cook's Note: I think these cookies taste their absolute best when fully cooled. I find that placing the just-baked cookies in the freezer for 5 to 10 minutes on a wire rack set over a baking sheet while still warm and gooey helps to dry out any excess grease and helps speed up the cooling process.

In a mixing bowl, whisk together the flour, kosher salt, baking powder, baking soda, and espresso powder, if using.

Add the flour mixture to the mixer bowl and mix until just combined. Add the chocolate and mix until incorporated. Transfer the dough to an airtight container and refrigerate for a minimum of 2 hours or up to overnight.

Preheat the oven to 350°F. Line a baking sheet with parchment paper.

Use a large spoon or ice cream scoop to shape into balls using 2 to 3 tablespoons of the dough. Place about 6 cookies on the prepared baking sheet, evenly spaced apart. Sprinkle each with flaky sea salt or fleur de sel. Transfer to the freezer for 10 to 15 minutes while the oven preheats.

Bake for about 10 to 12 minutes, until the edges are browned and set but the center still appears undercooked. Let the cookies cool on the baking sheet for 1 to 2 minutes then use a spatula to transfer the cookies to a wire rack to cool completely.

Prep Time: 5 minutes,
plus chilling time
Cook Time: 50 minutes,
plus cooling time

Creamy Rice Pudding

This rice pudding is one of my mom's traditional Christmas Eve desserts. Made with arborio rice and cooked slowly over the stovetop, it is super rich and creamy, but not too heavy. In fact, I generally convince myself on Christmas morning that it's wholesome enough to eat for breakfast. Word to the wise, though—do not leave the simmering pot of milk unattended or you may burn the milk. I know, it's a long time to stay near the stove on stirring duty, but each stir is working to guarantee a silkier and creamier rice pudding than others you may have tried before.

2 teaspoons spiced rum

½ cup golden raisins

1 quart whole milk

½ cup dry arborio rice

1 cinnamon stick
(or ¼ teaspoon ground
cinnamon)

Pinch of kosher salt

1 egg and 1 egg yolk,
lightly beaten

½ cup granulated sugar

1 tablespoon vanilla bean
paste or vanilla extract

½ cup heavy cream

Pinch of ground cinnamon,
for garnish (optional)

In a small bowl, pour the rum over the raisins and toss to combine. Set aside.

In a large heavy saucepan or Dutch oven set over medium heat, add the milk, rice, cinnamon stick, and salt. Bring to a boil, stirring frequently. Turn down the heat to low and continue to simmer, stirring frequently, for 40 to 45 minutes, until the rice has softened and absorbed most of the milk. Remove and discard the cinnamon stick.

In a bowl, whisk together the egg and egg yolk, sugar, and vanilla bean paste. Add the egg mixture to the rice mixture, and increase the heat to medium-low. Cook while stirring for about 2 minutes, until thickened. Add the heavy cream to the rice mixture and stir until combined, about 1 minute. Remove the pan from the heat and gently stir in the rum-flavored raisins.

Pour the rice pudding into a large serving bowl or individual serving dishes and cover with plastic wrap, placing the plastic wrap directly on the surface of the pudding. Let cool at room temperature for about 30 minutes, then refrigerate until cold, about 6 hours, or up to 3 days if making ahead. Serve chilled and garnish with a pinch of ground cinnamon, if desired.

Prep Time: 30 minutes,
plus a minimum of
6 hours chilling time
Cook Time: 25 minutes

Caramel Cheesecake Jars

No one can pass up these adorable and irresistibly creamy individually portioned desserts. The canning jars add a homey touch and enable you to see the delectable layers; they also add the convenience of being able to cover them with lids if making ahead, but small ramekins will work just as well.

1 cup finely crushed
shortbread cookies

2 tablespoons salted
butter, melted

2 tablespoons
confectioners' sugar

1 pound cream cheese,
at room temperature

½ cup granulated sugar

¼ cup store-bought sea
salt caramel sauce, at room
temperature, plus more
for serving

1 tablespoon heavy cream,
at room temperature

½ teaspoon vanilla extract

2 eggs plus 1 egg yolk, at
room temperature

Whipped Cream (page 191)

Preheat the oven to 325°F.

To make the shortbread crust, add the crushed cookies, melted butter, and confectioners' sugar to a small mixing bowl and toss with a fork until well combined. Divide the mixture among four half-pint wide-mouth canning jars (or four 6- to 8-ounce ramekins) and press down lightly until the crust layer is about ½ inch thick and climbs slightly up the sides of the jar.

In a stand mixer fitted with the paddle attachment, beat the cream cheese on medium-low for 3 minutes, until softened and creamy. Add the granulated sugar and beat until smooth. Add the caramel, heavy cream, and vanilla and mix until incorporated. Add the eggs and egg yolk, one at a time, scraping down the sides and bottom of the bowl after each addition, and mix on low speed until well combined.

Evenly divide the batter among the shortbread crust–filled jars. Prepare a water bath by placing the jars, evenly spaced, in a 9 by 13-inch baking pan. Carefully fill the baking pan with hot water so that the water level is halfway up the side of the jar. Very carefully transfer the baking pan to the oven.

Bake for 20 to 30 minutes, until the center is almost set and still jiggles slightly in the middle. Carefully remove the baking pan from the oven and let the jars cool in the water bath until cool enough to safely transfer the jars to a wire rack to cool completely. Cover with jar lids or plastic wrap and refrigerate for at least 6 hours.

Serve the cheesecakes chilled, topped with whipped cream and drizzled with caramel sauce.

Chocolate-Chocolate Cake with Fresh Raspberries

Can a chocolate cake, deep and dark in flavor and light in texture, with creamy, tangy chocolate frosting, be considered a guilt-free and healthy dessert when topped with fresh raspberries? That's the story that I'm going with. This cake is just the thing for birthdays or a new job or any milestone that deserves to be celebrated.

Frosting

2 ounces bittersweet dark chocolate (60–70 percent cacao), finely chopped

¾ cup unsweetened Dutch-process cocoa powder

¾ cup heavy cream

2 tablespoons crème fraîche or sour cream, at room temperature

2 tablespoons unsalted butter, at room temperature

2 teaspoons light corn syrup

1 teaspoon vanilla extract

1½ to 2 cups sifted confectioners' sugar, depending on consistency of frosting

Pinch of salt

Cake

1⅓ cups (160 grams) all-purpose flour

1½ teaspoons baking powder

½ teaspoon baking soda

¼ teaspoon kosher salt

½ cup 100 percent cacao unsweetened Dutch-processed cocoa powder

To make the chocolate frosting: Add the chopped chocolate to a large heatproof bowl. Sift or use a fine-mesh sieve to add in the cocoa powder. Set aside.

In a small heavy saucepan over medium heat, add the heavy cream, crème fraîche, and butter, and bring to a simmer, whisking frequently, until just starting to release steam. Pour the hot cream mixture over the chocolate-cocoa mixture and let sit for about 5 minutes. Whisk until well combined and smooth. Stir in the corn syrup and vanilla and set aside to cool until tepid (90°F to 110°F).

Add 1½ cups of the confectioners' sugar and salt and whisk until smooth and well combined. Add additional confectioners' sugar in ¼-cup increments until the consistency of the frosting is thick and spreadable. (The frosting will get firmer as it cools.)

Cover and let the frosting cool to room temperature before using. If you're making it more than 2 or 3 hours ahead, store it in an airtight container in the refrigerator until ready to use, up to 1 week. Use the frosting at room temperature for best results.

To make the cake: Preheat the oven to 350°F. Butter the bottom and sides of two 6-inch round cake pans (or one loaf pan) and line the bottom of each pan with a piece of parchment paper cut to fit inside.

In a large bowl, add the flour, baking powder, baking soda, and salt. Sift or use a fine-mesh sieve to add in the cocoa powder, then whisk until evenly combined. Set aside.

In a separate bowl, whisk together the buttermilk, coffee, and vanilla. Set aside.

CONTINUED

Chocolate-Chocolate Cake with Fresh Raspberries

¾ cup buttermilk

⅓ cup strong brewed coffee (or ½ teaspoon espresso powder dissolved in ⅓ cup water)

1 teaspoon vanilla extract

2 eggs

1¼ cups granulated sugar

½ cup canola oil (or vegetable oil)

Fresh raspberries, for topping

In a stand mixer fitted with the whisk attachment, whisk the eggs and granulated sugar on high speed until pale yellow and thickened, about 5 minutes. Turn the mixer down to low, slowly pour in the oil, and mix until just combined.

Switch over to the paddle attachment and, with the mixer on low speed, add the buttermilk mixture and mix until the batter is smooth and evenly combined, about 2 minutes. Add the flour mixture and mix until no dry flour is visible, scraping the sides and bottom of the bowl with a spatula as needed.

Pour the batter into the prepared cake pans. Bake for about 30 minutes, or until a cake tester inserted into the center comes out clean. Let cool on a wire rack in the pan. Once cool, carefully remove the cakes from the pan, pulling away and discarding the parchment paper.

To assemble: If making the 6-inch round cake, use an offset spatula to spread one-third of the frosting on top of one of the cakes, edge to edge. Place the other cake on top of the frosting and press it down lightly to stick, making sure the cake is level. Frost the top and sides with the remaining frosting.

If making the loaf cake, slice the cake horizontally in three even layers and frost the top of each of the first two layers with one-quarter of the frosting, then stack and press them down lightly to stick, making sure the cake is level. Frost the top and sides of the cake with the remaining frosting until completely covered.

Top with fresh raspberries and serve.

Churros with Mexican-Style Chocolate Sauce

If you have never made churros at home, you will be surprised at how wonderful they taste when they are warm and fresh. When fried at the right temperature, they come out light and crisp and absorb a minimum amount of oil. Using a large pastry bag with a large star-piping tip (about ½-inch opening—Ateco 846 or Wilton 1M) is essential in forming the ridges that give the churro its signature crispy exterior. Purchasing a star-piping tip is well worth the modest investment; it can be found at most craft stores. You can also use the tip to make a superior-looking frosted cupcake.

Churros are an ideal recipe to make as a team, as it takes some practice to be able to swiftly pipe and cut the dough into the hot oil by yourself. Have your partner lend you a hand when it comes time for frying—one person pipes, the other person cuts. While one person monitors the frying, the other can be the designated cinnamon-sugar roller and taste taster. The churros might even disappear as fast as you make them.

Chocolate Sauce

3 ounces dark chocolate, preferably stone-ground Mexican-style, finely chopped

⅔ cup heavy cream

1 tablespoon unsweetened cocoa powder

½ teaspoon espresso powder

2 teaspoons Kahlúa

Pinch of kosher salt

Pinch of ground cinnamon (optional)

To make the chocolate sauce: Add the chocolate to a medium (completely dry) heatproof bowl. In a small saucepan over medium heat, add the heavy cream and bring to a simmer. Add the cocoa powder, espresso powder, Kahlúa, salt, and cinnamon, if using. Return to a simmer while whisking to completely dissolve the cocoa and espresso powders. Pour the warm cream mixture over the chopped chocolate and let it sit for 3 to 4 minutes. Then whisk until the chocolate is completely melted and smooth. Keep warm. (If making ahead, store in an airtight container in the refrigerator for up to 5 days. Warm in a saucepan over low heat until melted and stir until smooth.)

To make the churros: Mix ½ cup of the sugar and the cinnamon in a shallow dish and set aside.

Line a baking sheet with paper towels and set aside.

Fit a large pastry bag with a large star-piping tip and place it in a tall glass, cuffing the top of the pastry bag over the glass.

CONTINUED

CONTINUED

Churros with Mexican-Style Chocolate Sauce

Churros

½ cup plus 1 tablespoon granulated sugar

1½ teaspoons ground cinnamon

¾ cup water

6 tablespoons unsalted butter

1 teaspoon vanilla extract

¼ teaspoon salt

¾ cup (90 grams) all-purpose flour

2 eggs

Canola oil, for frying

Cook's Notes: Assemble all the necessary ingredients and equipment before heating the oil. A frying or candy thermometer will take the guesswork out of maintaining the ideal frying temperature (360°F), which fluctuates as each batch is added.

Test the first churro for timing to ensure an evenly browned, crispy exterior and fully cooked, slightly hollow interior.

In a saucepan over high heat, add the remaining 1 tablespoon of sugar, the water, butter, vanilla, and salt, stirring until the sugar dissolves. Bring to a boil. Turn the heat down to medium and add the flour all at once, stirring vigorously with a wooden spoon, until fully incorporated and the batter transforms into a cohesive, thick dough that pulls away from the sides of the pan. Lower the heat and stir the dough for an additional 1 to 2 minutes, until a thin film coats the bottom of the pan.

Remove the pan from the heat to cool slightly, 3 to 5 minutes, stirring occasionally to encourage cooling. Gradually add one egg at a time, stirring vigorously with a wooden spoon after each addition until completely incorporated. Continue to stir until the dough becomes a somewhat sticky paste with a slight gloss. The paste should be pipeable—not too thick and not too runny.

Using a spoon or spatula, transfer the dough to the pastry bag. Twist and fold down the top of bag and secure with a rubber band.

Heat 1½ inches of canola oil in a heavy skillet over high heat until the oil temperature reaches 360°F.

Working carefully, pipe lines of dough about 6 inches long into the hot oil, cutting the ends with a paring knife or scissors. (The lines are not going to be perfectly straight—this is fine!) Working in batches of 3, allow them to fry for 3 to 4 minutes, turning halfway through, until they are evenly golden brown and fully cooked in the center. Carefully remove the churros with tongs, allowing the excess oil to drip back into skillet. Place them on the paper towel–lined baking sheet to drain. When cool enough to handle, roll the churros in the cinnamon-sugar mixture.

Serve warm with the warm chocolate sauce for dipping.

If making ahead, fry and drain the churros but do not roll them in the cinnamon-sugar mixture. Let cool completely, then store in an airtight container in the freezer for up to 1 week. Reheat the churros, wrapped in foil, in a 350°F oven for about 15 minutes, or until warm. Roll the churros in the cinnamon-sugar mixture while still warm.

Cocktails for Couples

by Kara Newman

A well-made cocktail is an ideal way to ease into a meal or toast a special moment. Somehow it seems to add a certain warmth and intimacy to a memory you're creating: the martini that flanks the appetizers while dinner cooks; a hot toddy warming your fingers as you curl up by the fireplace on a blustery evening; or a pitcher of margaritas enjoyed outdoors with friends, maybe while the grill preheats.

The point is, you don't have to go to a bar to have a good cocktail. The culture of cocktails has shifted as more people are entertaining at home. At the same time, excellent spirits, mixers, and tools for making drinks have become more widely available. Even more important: In recent years, bartenders and other experts have widely shared their knowledge about how to make cocktails. All this adds up to better cocktails at home, whether enjoying a solitary dram, celebrating as a couple, or hosting a full-on dinner party.

All of the drinks on the following pages are designed to be mixed in duplicate; many are easy to scale up for cocktail parties or other gatherings.

Basic Bar Equipment

The truth is, you don't need much. A **jigger** will ensure accurate measurements of liquid ingredients; the most versatile jigger measures 1 ounce on one side and 2 ounces on the other.

A **mixing glass** is used for stirred drinks that contain no juice, such as martinis; a **cocktail shaker** is used to incorporate juice into shaken drinks, such as daiquiris and margaritas. Other accoutrements include a long-handled **barspoon** for stirring and a **strainer** for holding back ice.

GLASSWARE

Showcase drinks in stemmed glasses, such as V-shaped **martini glasses** or shallow bowl-shaped **coupes**. Holding these glasses by the stem help keep drinks colder longer, since you're not cupping them in your warm hands. Delicate **champagne flutes** also have stems.

Lowball glasses such as **rocks glasses** and **old-fashioned glasses** also are useful for holding drinks served with ice, particularly those with large chunks of ice.

"Long" drinks are usually topped up with mixers and often are served over plenty of ice. Serve them in **tall**

highball glasses, such as a Collins glass. Frozen drinks can be served in highballs, though the hourglass-shaped **hurricane glass** is also a popular choice.

Basic Spirits

You don't need to buy out the entire liquor store— if you're building a bar from scratch, start with three spirits, one bottle of vermouth, and perhaps one liqueur.

CORE SPIRITS

Gin: Usually a good choice is London Dry, which means that it has a strong dose of pinelike juniper. You'll want a bottle for mixing martinis, gin and tonics, and negronis.

Whiskey: Choose either bourbon, rye whiskey, and/ or Scotch whisky. Unless you already know that you love super-smoky whiskey, opt for a mellow, versatile whiskey to start out your bar. Bourbon, made with at least 51 percent corn, will be a bit sweeter, while rye whiskey, made with at least 51 percent rye grain, will be a bit spicier. Scotch—shorthand for Scotland's native whisky, made from malted barley—is usually a good choice for straight-up sipping.

Vodka: Use for bloody Marys and Moscow mules or for martini-style cocktails if you prefer vodka over gin.

Tequila: Look for a bottle that says "100 percent agave" on the label. Blanco (unaged/minimally aged) tequilas are crisp and good for mixing; reposado (aged less than one year) tequilas tend to have gentle vanilla or honey notes and can be sipped or mixed.

Rum: Aged or white rum, whichever you prefer, is for mixing into daiquiris, piña coladas, and tropical drinks. White rum is usually a classic for mixing, while aged rums can double as straight-up sippers if you enjoy rich brown sugar or caramel notes.

Brandy: Select something you enjoy sipping straight but isn't too expensive for mixing into cocktails such as sidecars or brandy Alexanders. A VSOP Cognac or Armagnac is usually a solid choice; VSOP means it's blended from a mix of brandies, and the youngest in the blend at least four years old. VS is made with a mix of younger brandies and may be too harsh to sip straight, while XO brandies can be pricey—a nice treat but not recommended for mixing.

WINE

Vermouth: Dry (white) vermouth is ideal for martinis, while sweet (red) vermouth is used in manhattans and negronis. Be sure to refrigerate vermouth once it's opened.

Champagne or other sparkling wine: Champagne refers to sparkling wine made in France's Champagne region. It's delightful, but it's not the only sparkling wine available: Prosecco, Cava, and domestic sparklers all can be used to add effervescence to cocktails—or of, course, to sip straight.

Sherry: This is a fortified wine from Spain's Jerez region, and comes in a wide array of flavor profiles, from dry and crisp to sweeter and raisin-y. Opt for the former in cocktails like the Adonis (page 224).

LIQUEURS

In addition to adding flavor to cocktails, the following liqueurs can be consumed on their own as a small pour, either as an *aperitivo* or a dessert.

> A good amaro or two (Averna, Ramazzotti, and Nonino all are highly recommended)
> Campari or another "red bitter"
> Cointreau or another orange liqueur
> Crème de cacao

Mixers

The following nonalcoholic ingredients, in addition to lemon juice and lime juice, are used to mix the cocktails on the following pages.

> Sparkling mixers, such as tonic water, soda water, or seltzer
> Ginger beer (which can be mixed with a spirit of choice and ice for a simple highball)
> Grapefruit soda (for palomas)
> Fruit and vegetable juices, such as grapefruit, tomato, and pineapple

Sweeteners, Garnishes, and More

These additions add finesse to many drinks.

SYRUPS

Simple syrup isn't difficult to make: In a saucepan, combine equal parts hot water and sugar and stir until the sugar dissolves. Remove from the heat and, when cooled, decant into a container with a lid and keep in the refrigerator for up to two weeks. Drinks also can be sweetened with agave nectar, maple syrup, honey, or honey syrup (a mix of two parts honey and one part hot water).

GARNISHES

The purpose of a garnish is to add visual appeal and also to entice with a pleasing aroma and maybe a hint of flavor.

Citrus peels (also called twists): Use a peeler to cut away a swath of lemon, lime, orange, or grapefruit peel. Choose a thicker peel to accentuate a sturdy drink in a rocks glass or use a knife to cut a thinner peel for a more delicate coupe or champagne flute.

Wedges: Cut lemons or limes into quarters.

Brandied cherries: Whenever possible, use brandied cherries rather than supersweet artificially colored maraschino cherries. Try making a batch when cherries are in season (many recipes can be found online), or purchase a brand like Luxardo.

Spices: Raid the spice rack for whole spices to garnish cocktails. Spices called for in this chapter include nutmeg (grate from a whole nutmeg, if possible), cinnamon sticks, and star anise.

Whether dashed into a cocktail to add subtle flavor or dotted on top like a garnish, bitters will round out your bar cart. Start with two must-have bottles: spiced **Angostura**, which is essential for old-fashioneds and manhattans, and **orange bitters**, which add enticing aromatics to martinis.

A Word about Ice

While the following drink recipes keep things simple and call mostly for cubed ice, for special occasions, you may want to experiment with crushed ice (ideal for tropical drinks like the piña colada) or large cubes or spheres (ideal for strong and stirred drinks that you'll want to sip slowly, such as the boulevardier.)

How to Host: Party Planning Tips

The basic rule of thumb: If you're having fun, your guests will be, too. The secrets to remaining relaxed?

PLAN AHEAD

For drinks, that means stealing a page from restaurant and bar playbooks: Be sure to practice *mise en place* in your bar, a French culinary term that means "putting in place."

Make sure all of your bottles, glassware, ice, and cleanup gear is close at hand (position a trash bin near the bar, too). Anything that can be made or mixed ahead of time should be—that means citrus is juiced, garnishes are precut, and ingredients are premeasured when possible. At the last minute, you can simply pour, chill, garnish—and then relax with your guests.

BE COOL ABOUT ICE

You can never have too much ice. But how much is enough? Try this bartender formula: For each 750 ml of cocktail (the size of a standard bottle of liquor), allot 7 pounds of ice. Then add extra, especially if you're planning to set out tubs to chill bottled cocktails (more on that below), wine, or sodas.

PREBATCH DRINKS

For easy serving, try making a big batch of one of these drinks. They scale up well, so you can make them before your guests arrive. If you're hosting

as a couple, consider dividing the duties behind the bar—one person mixes and pours, for example, while the other garnishes and hands the finished drink to the thirsty guest.

Bottled Cocktails

In general, spirit-forward cocktails (which contain little or no juice) work best for bottled drinks. To make bottled cocktails for 10-12 guests: First, multiply the ingredients by the number of guests. In a large pitcher, combine the ingredients, plus ½ cup of ice (this mimics the dilution that ice would provide). Stir to combine, then decant into clean wine bottles – most recipes will fit into two or three 750-ml bottles. Chill the bottles in the refrigerator for at least 2 hours and stash them in a bucket of ice during the party. When ready to serve, pour directly into coupe glasses, with no additional ice. Serves 10 to 12.

Try this with:

Manhattans/Black Manhattans (page 215)
Martinis/50-50 Martinis (page 215)
Negronis (page 216)
Adonis/Bamboo (page 224)

Pitcher Drinks

Cocktails with lots of fruit and fizz are relatively forgiving in pitcher format. To make pitcher drinks for 10 to 12 guests: First, multiply the ingredients by the number of guests. In a large pitcher (or divided evenly among two smaller pitchers), combine the ingredients and stir to combine. Add the ice at the very last minute (or scoop ice directly into glasses instead of the pitcher) to avoid watered-down drinks, and stir again to chill. Serves 10 to 12.

Try this with:

Margaritas (page 216)
Bloody Marys (page 219)
Daiquiris (page 220)
French 75s (page 225)
Palomas (page 223)

MANHATTAN

DAIQUIRI

BRANDY ALEXANDER

HOT TODDY

MARTINI

FRENCH 75

PALOMA

MARGARITA

Martini

The martini is a highly personal drink. Some people prefer the softening touch of extra vermouth; others want a stiff sipper with as little vermouth as possible. Some want to garnish with a twist of lemon, and others garnish with an olive or three. This recipe is a starting point and by all means should be adjusted to accommodate your personal taste. One nonnegotiable: A good martini should always be served as icy cold as possible. (Bonus: It never hurts to set the glass in the freezer to chill.) MAKES 2 DRINKS

6 ounces gin

2 ounces dry vermouth

4 dashes orange bitters (optional)

2 lemon peels or olives, for garnish

Combine the gin, vermouth, and bitters (if using) in a mixing glass with ice. Stir well to chill, then strain into two martini or coupe glasses. Garnish each glass with a lemon peel or olive.

VARIATION: 50-50 MARTINI

As the name suggests, it's 50 percent gin, 50 percent vermouth.

Combine 3 ounces each of gin and dry vermouth and add 4 dashes of orange bitters (if using) in a mixing glass with ice. Stir well to chill, then strain into two martini or coupe glasses. Garnish each glass with a lemon peel.

VARIATION: REVERSE MARTINI

This is a low-octane version of the classic martini; it has been noted as a Julia Child–favored aperitif.

Combine 6 ounces dry vermouth and 2 ounces gin in a mixing glass with ice. Stir well to chill, then strain into two martini or coupe glasses. Garnish each glass with a lemon peel or olive.

Manhattan

This classic sipper is traditionally made with lean, spicy rye whiskey, but there's nothing wrong with subbing in bourbon if that's your go-to pour. It's also a malleable drink that lends itself to variations, such as the amaro-spiked black manhattan. MAKES 2 DRINKS

4 ounces rye whiskey

2 ounce sweet vermouth

4 dashes Angostura bitters

Brandied cherries, for garnish (see page 211)

In a mixing glass, stir together the rye whiskey, sweet vermouth, and bitters with ice. Strain into two chilled coupe glasses. Garnish each glass with a cherry.

VARIATION: BLACK MANHATTAN

This was originally created by bartender Todd Smith for the San Francisco bar Bourbon and Branch. If you don't have Averna amaro on hand, try Ramazzotti or any other amaro with a bit of sweetness to it.

In a mixing glass, stir together 4 ounces rye whiskey, 2 ounces Averna amaro, and 2 dashes each Angostura and orange bitters with ice. Strain into two chilled coupe glasses and garnish each glass with a cherry.

Margarita

No wonder the margarita is one of the most popular cocktails in the world. When done right, the simple trinity of tequila, fresh lime juice, and orange liqueur is potent, refreshing, and ideal for celebrating. MAKES 2 DRINKS

Coarse salt, to rim the glass

Lime wedges, to rim the glass

4 ounces silver tequila

2 ounces Cointreau or other orange liqueur

2 ounces fresh lime juice

Place the salt in a dish. Moisten the edge of two rocks glasses by rubbing the lime wedge around the rim, then roll the edge of each glass along the salt to coat.

In a cocktail shaker, combine the tequila, Cointreau, and lime juice with ice. Shake well, then strain into the prepared glasses over fresh ice.

TIPS TO CUSTOMIZE YOUR MARGARITA

An easy way to personalize your marg is to mix up a special salt blend for rimming the glasses, which adds flavor and a hint of color. Here are some combinations to try.

Piquant: Salt + black pepper

Spicy: Salt + cayenne pepper or chile powder

Fresh: Salt + finely chopped fresh herbs

Citrusy: Salt + finely chopped citrus peels

Sweet: Sugar + cocoa powder

Negroni

Think of this ruby-hued drink as an excuse to indulge in Italy's *aperitivo* hour, complete with small but good things to eat and plenty of cocktails made with bracingly bitter amaro. Here, Campari provides the striking red hue as well as the bracingly bitter edge that's ideal for setting the mouth watering and stoking the appetite. MAKES 2 DRINKS

2 ounces gin

2 ounces sweet vermouth

2 ounces Campari

Soda water, to top (optional)

2 lemon peels, for garnish

Divide the gin, sweet vermouth, and Campari between two rocks glasses. Scoop ice into each glass and stir to chill. Top up with soda water, if desired. Garnish each glass with a lemon peel.

VARIATION: BOULEVARDIER

Exchange the gin for bourbon. Where the negroni is ideal for warm-weather drinks, the boulevardier is a hardier cousin suited for sipping when the mercury drops.

In a mixing glass, stir together 2 ounces each of bourbon, sweet vermouth, and Campari with ice. Strain into two rocks glasses, each with a large cube of ice. Garnish each glass with an orange peel.

MOSCOW MULE

PINA COLADA

BLOODY MARY

ADONIS

Bloody Mary

Whether for brunch for two or a weekend with the extended tribe, there's nothing like a bloody Mary to start things off right. For a group get-together, consider setting up a bloody Mary bar: Start with a pitcher of your own house bloody mix, bottles of vodka (or tequila or cachaça, if preferred), and—most important—an over-the-top selection of garnishes to skewer, stir, and nibble. MAKES 2 DRINKS

3 ounces vodka

6 ounces tomato juice

1 ounce fresh lemon juice

4 dashes Worcestershire sauce

2 dashes Tabasco sauce

Pinch of celery salt

Pinch of freshly ground pepper

Garnishes, as desired (see suggestions below)

In a mixing glass or carafe, mix together the vodka, tomato juice, lemon juice, Worcestershire, Tabasco, celery salt, and pepper. Pour into two Collins glasses filled with ice. Don't skimp on the garnishes—excess is encouraged!

GARNISH BAR SUGGESTIONS
Grated horseradish, celery ribs, cucumber spears, caperberries or cornichons, blue cheese–stuffed olives, pickled vegetables, fresh herb sprigs (such as basil or cilantro), lemon and lime wedges, radishes, crisp bacon, cooked and peeled shrimp

Moscow Mule

The hallmark of this popular vodka drink is the shiny copper mug—but it's not required. This drink can easily be built in a tall Collins glass or a generous size rocks glass instead. MAKES 2 DRINKS

1 lime, cut in half

4 ounces vodka

6 ounces ginger beer, or more if desired

Squeeze the juice from each lime half into a copper Moscow Mule mug (it should yield about ½ ounce lime juice per drink). Drop the spent lime hull into each mug. Divide the vodka between the mugs. Scoop in ice and stir to chill. Top up with ginger beer.

VARIATION: KENTUCKY MULE
Same instructions as above, but swap in 4 ounces of bourbon for the vodka. Garnish each mug with a sprig of mint.

Daiquiri

Forget about the slushy frozen daiquiris seen on cruise ships and at vacation resorts. The real daiq is essentially a fresh, bracing rum sour, stripped down to its elegant core. This is the version served by any bartender who ever worked with the late bartending legend Sasha Petraske, perfected to three elements, and presented unadorned. MAKES 2 DRINKS

4 ounces white rum

2 ounces fresh lime juice

1½ ounces simple syrup (1 part sugar to 1 part water; see page 211)

In a cocktail shaker, combine the rum, lime juice, and simple syrup with large ice cubes. Shake vigorously and strain into two coupe glasses.

Brandy Alexander

This decadent, dessertlike drink is a tradition at many holiday tables. Since brandy is the key ingredient, select a good bottle of Cognac or Armagnac. It makes all the difference in how the drink turns out—plus it gives something nice to pour as a post-post-dessert nightcap. MAKES 2 DRINKS

2½ ounces brandy

2 ounces crème de cacao

1½ ounces heavy cream

Grated nutmeg or chocolate shavings, for garnish

In a cocktail shaker, combine the brandy, crème de cacao, and cream with ice. Shake well, and strain into two coupes or martini glasses. Garnish each glass with grated nutmeg or chocolate shavings.

Old-Fashioned

Part of the fun of making an old-fashioned is a spirited debate over which whiskey to choose: spicy rye or mellow bourbon? Whichever is preferred, know that this is a drink with plenty of history—and muscle—to it. Sip slowly and savor. MAKES 2 DRINKS

2 sugar cubes

4 dashes Angostura bitters

4 ounces rye or bourbon

2 orange peels, for garnish

In the bottom of each of two rocks glass, muddle 1 sugar cube, 2 dashes of bitters, and a barspoon of warm water until the sugar dissolves. Add 2 ounces rye or bourbon to each glass and stir to incorporate the sugar mixture. Add ice and stir to chill. Garnish each glass with an orange peel.

TIPS TO CUSTOMIZE YOUR OLD-FASHIONED

Although this classic cocktail appears austere, it's remarkably versatile, lending itself to all kinds of tweaks to suit any preference.

Switch the base. Switch bourbon for rye, or add 1 ounce of each; try blended Scotch, Japanese whiskey, or other types of whiskey; experiment with all the brown spirits: aged rum, añejo tequila, or brandy.

Use better bitters. The cinnamon-spice notes of Angostura are traditional, but the OF takes well to other accents, too. Try orange bitters, chocolate mole bitters, or the cherry-forward Peychaud's.

Game the garnish. A simple swath of orange peel is a classic touch, but lemon or grapefruit peels (or both!) add nuanced aroma and vary the visual pop of color in the glass. Quite a few people prefer their old-fashioneds with brandied cherries (see page 211), either in place of or in addition to the citrus peel garnish.

Gin & Tonic

The cool, crisp G&T can take many forms, from the buttoned-down classic that might serve as a refresher after a match on the tennis courts to the raucous, highly personalized gin-tonics popularized in Spain's late-night hotspots.

MAKES 2 DRINKS

4 ounces London Dry gin

1 lime, cut into quarters

6 to 8 ounces tonic water

Scoop ice into two Collins glasses. Pour 2 ounces gin into each glass. Squeeze 2 lime wedges into each glass, then drop the wedges in the glass. Top up each glass with 3 to 4 ounces tonic water. Stir to combine and chill.

VARIATION: GIN-TONIC

Consider setting up a gin-tonic bar for entertaining, since this is a drink meant to mix and match, an exercise involving multiple bottles. Set out one or more of the following:

Gin: Offer a classic London Dry gin, which will have plenty of pinelike juniper flavor (such as Tanqueray); a more neutral gin (such as Plymouth); and a "wild card" gin that has unusual flavorings (such as Hendrick's, which has pronounced floral and cucumber notes).

Tonic: A classic tonic is fine; consider also splurging on a specialty tonic (such as Fever Tree or Q Tonic) and, to gild the lily, add a tonic syrup (such as Tom's Tonic).

Garnishes: And plenty of them—wheels of citrus, sprigs of fresh herbs, cucumber slices, berries or other fresh fruit, and spices such as cardamom or anise.

In each large wine glass or snifter, scoop in ice, then add 2 ounces of the gin of choice, topped up with 3 to 4 ounces of the tonic of choice. Garnish generously.

Paloma

In Mexico, margaritas are strictly for the beach; palomas are the preferred way to drink tequila. At heart, the paloma is a straightforward, highball-style cocktail, just an ounce or two of tequila topped up with grapefruit-flavored soda and perhaps a squeeze of lime, all poured over ice without fanfare. If you can find Squirt or Jarritos grapefruit soda, that's ideal; if not, mix grapefruit juice and club soda with a spoonful of sugar. MAKES 2 DRINKS

Coarse salt and lime wedges,
to rim the glass (optional)

4 ounces tequila

1 ounce fresh lime juice

Grapefruit soda (like Squirt or Jarritos), to top

2 grapefruit slices or lime wedges, for garnish

Place the salt in a dish, if using. Moisten the edge of two rocks glasses by rubbing the lime wedge around the rim, then roll the edge of each glass along the salt to coat.

Fill each glass with ice. Add 2 ounces tequila and ½ ounce lime juice to each glass, then top each with grapefruit soda. Stir gently to mix and chill. Garnish each glass with a grapefruit slice or lime wedge.

Adonis

Sherry plus vermouth equals a low-alcohol cocktail that's easy to make and easy to drink. One simple switch—from sweet vermouth to dry vermouth—turns the Adonis into a bamboo.

MAKES 2 DRINKS

4 ounces fino sherry

4 ounces sweet vermouth

4 dashes orange bitters

Orange peels, for garnish

In a mixing glass, combine the sherry, vermouth, and bitters with ice. Stir well, then strain into two coupe glasses. Garnish each glass with an orange peel.

VARIATION: BAMBOO

In a mixing glass, combine 4 ounces sherry, 4 ounces dry vermouth, and 2 dashes each of orange and Angostura bitters. Stir with ice, then strain into two coupe glasses. Garnish each glass with a lemon peel.

Hot Toddy

Beloved for chasing off chills and warding off colds, hot toddies are a warming winter favorite. Although the classic is made with little more than whiskey, lemon, honey, and hot water, this drink is easy to customize, based on what's handy in the home bar and the pantry. Just a few tweaks can lead to the creation of your own special house hot toddy. MAKES 2 DRINKS

3 ounces whiskey

2 tablespoons honey

1 ounce fresh lemon juice

2 cups hot water

2 lemon wedges and/or cinnamon sticks, for garnish

Warm two mugs by rinsing them with hot water. In each mug, stir together 1½ ounces whiskey, 1 tablespoon honey, ½ ounce lemon juice, and 1 cup hot water. Garnish each mug with a lemon wedge and/or cinnamon stick.

TIPS TO CUSTOMIZE YOUR HOT TODDY

- Swap out whiskey for another brown liquor, such as brandy, rum, or applejack.

- Instead of honey, sweeten with maple syrup, demerara syrup, or brown sugar.

- Add flavor with chai tea, splashes of amaro, or dashes of bitters.

- Adjust the garnishes: Try star anise, curls of orange peel, or grated nutmeg.

Piña Colada

Break out the blender! This iconic drink was created at San Juan's Caribe Hilton. There's some debate as to who exactly created the drink, but in general the nod goes to Ramon "Monchito" Marrero Perez, one of the Caribe Hilton's early local bartenders, in 1954. As the story goes, Perez spent three months experimenting before he finally created a drink he felt captured "the sunny, tropical flavors of Puerto Rico in a glass."

MAKES 2 DRINKS

4 ounces white rum, preferably Puerto Rican rum

2 ounces coconut cream

2 ounces heavy cream

12 ounces fresh pineapple juice

2 cups crushed ice

2 fresh pineapple wedges and maraschino cherries, for garnish

In a blender, combine the rum, coconut cream, heavy cream, pineapple juice, and crushed ice. Blend for about 15 seconds, or until smooth. Pour into two hurricane glasses. Garnish each glass with a pineapple wedge and cherries.

French 75

The original recipe for this festive fizz called for Cognac, but today, most bartenders make their 75s with gin. What doesn't change? A generous pour of sparkling wine, which makes this drink perfect for all kinds of celebratory occasions.

A word of warning: This innocent-looking cocktail was named after a light-but-powerful French gun used in World War I—a not-so-subtle nod to the drink's lethalness. It's beautiful, but it packs a punch. MAKES 2 DRINKS

2½ ounces gin

⅔ ounce fresh lemon juice

½ ounce simple syrup (1 part sugar to 1 part water; see page 211)

5 ounces brut Champagne or other dry sparkling wine

2 lemon peels, for garnish

Combine the gin, lemon juice, and simple syrup in a cocktail shaker with ice. Shake well, then strain into two champagne flutes. Top up each glass with Champagne. Twist a lemon peel over each glass to express the essential oils from the skin, then use the peel to garnish.

Acknowledgments

To Jeanette, for being such an invaluable partner in developing and testing the recipes for this book. Your boundless enthusiasm and support always gave us the push we needed.

Thank you Jimmy for sharing your genius recipes and Vicki for devoting your time to us in so many ways. And to our parents, whose passion for creating happy memories around the table are undeniably at the heart of this whole book.

To our siblings who are always there for us with their love and continue to be our greatest champions. Your endorsement is our security blanket and most treasured asset.

To Jason and Emily Kan, for lending us light in the dark hours of this project, literally and figuratively. To all of our friends—your optimism and encouragement always kept us moving in the right direction.

To Laura Lee at Present Perfect Dept. for being a source of professional wisdom and guidance with your calm, warm nature.

Thank you to Kelly Snowden, Emma Campion, Kim Keller, Mari Gill, and Dan Myers and everyone at Ten Speed who contributed their considerable talent and effort and to the creation of this book. Thank you for your trust, and for continuously valuing our perspective and vision for this project.

About the Authors

Kiera and Cole are a husband-and-wife creative team and the founders of Cole and Kiera Photography, a wedding and lifestyle photography business. Collaborating as a creative duo, they are the authors, stylists, and photographers of the *Ultimate Appetizer Ideabook* and their latest book, *The Couple's Cookbook*. Their recipes have been published in *Oprah* and *Redbook*. With a background and degree in business management, Kiera left the corporate world to pursue her passion for creating beautiful and delicious food, starting with her baking blog turned online cookie favor business, SweetKiera.com. Cole has a degree in graphic design, but his education in photography began in his father's darkroom when he was a boy. Cole and Kiera currently reside in the Boston area with two little ones with very healthy appetites—their French bulldog Georgia and their two-year-old daughter, Chloe.

Index

Ten Speed Press and the Ten Speed Press colophon are registered
trademarks of Penguin Random House LLC.

Library of Congress Cataloging-in-Publication Data
Names: Stipovich, Cole, author. | Stipovich, Kiera, author.
Title: The couple's cookbook : recipes for newlyweds /
   by Cole and Kiera Stipovich.
Description: Oakland, CA : Ten Speed Press, [2019]
Identifiers: LCCN 2019014811 | ISBN 9780399581465 (hardcover)
Subjects: LCSH: Cooking for two. | Newlyweds. | LCGFT: Cookbooks.
Classification: LCC TX652 .S76 2019 | DDC 641.5/61—dc23 LC record
   available at https://lccn.loc.gov/2019014811

Hardcover ISBN: 978-0-399-58146-5
eBook ISBN: 978-0-399-58147-2

Printed in China

Design by Emma Campion

10 9 8 7 6 5 4 3 2 1

First Edition